CHANGE
QUESTIONS

CHANGE QUESTIONS
A Playbook for Effective and Lasting Organizational Change

First Modus Cooperandi Press Edition: July 2023

ISBN: 978-0-9890812-9-0 (paperback)

Editor: Lex Schroeder
Layout: Olivier Darbonville
Copy Editor: Chet Marchwinski

For bulk copies, educational discounts, interviews or other inquiries, contact: changequestions.net

NO MORE FLAVOR OF THE MONTH

A PLAYBOOK FOR EFFECTIVE AND LASTING
ORGANIZATIONAL CHANGE

CHANGE QUESTIONS

D. LYNN KELLEY

WITH JOHN SHOOK

Contents

Chapter 9 contains the Change Questions guide. The guide gives practical information on how to use the Change Questions.

If you are the kind of person who wants to skip the stories, examples, and theories, you can jump right into the Change Questions through the digital workbook which gives you access to the forms, outlines, meeting agendas, and examples described in this book. Feel free to use the fillable pdf format in the digital workbook with your team when planning a Change Initiative. Use the following link or QR code to access the digital workbook.

changequestions.net

Foreword

In 2010 at Union Pacific (UP), I had just been named executive vice president, operations, the chief operating job in the railroad. I was very familiar with the network, having been responsible for two operating regions as well as labor relations. We had been continuously improving operations over time—better service, more efficient, safer. But we were certain we could be much more. There was tension between how we were performing and how we could perform. The question was "How can we be better? How can we improve employee engagement, customer satisfaction, safety performance, and operating results, simultaneously?" And the employee part of the equation was perhaps most important—change lasts when people buy into it. To get buy-in there had to be a hook—"what's in it for me?" I believed the answer to that question was fulfillment, respect, and feeling valued.

As an iconic industrial and Fortune 200 leader in the United States, UP was doing okay in 2010. The 2008 Financial Crisis had prompted a significant freight recession, and our volumes were down, putting the business under pressure. But it wasn't a burning platform. In that environment, we needed to think about both the present *and* our future. How could we build fundamental improvement processes into the business, deeply seated, so every team had the tools necessary to make their work safer, more efficient, with better outcomes, every day? All while trimming costs to match our decline in volumes? The Change Questions, which are customizable given your business situation and context, provided a guide to accomplish this at UP in a way that would bring the entire team along.

Leading change in organizations is just plain hard. Inspiring people and getting them engaged in change work that is sustained is even harder. But I knew Lean operating principles could help and I knew I had a partner in Lynn Kelley. Lynn knew the principles and how to intrinsically motivate employees. She had the right experience, track record, and leadership skills to be a great partner.

We chose to implement the Change Questions in a planned, targeted way. We rejected a "peanut butter" approach, in which we would train everyone, all at once, with the tools – and then hope they took hold. Instead, we started small, focusing on teams that were hungry and ready, and measured their engagement and results over time. The Change Questions came to life for me when I saw their power to transform our daily grind—improvement driven by the individuals doing the work. The tools worked if implemented properly and matured. Over the past twelve years, we have continued to expand and mature, at this point training and graduating roughly 200 Lean practitioners each year who operate teams under the Lean principles.

My hope is that you will use *Change Questions* to transform your own businesses, organizations, or institutions. I encourage you to be deliberate—you might be a zealot, but that doesn't matter if your team doesn't understand or buy into the effort. There always must be a what's-in-it-for-me element in change management. Using the Change Questions is an empowerment tool—the team members who do the work have the intellectual capital to make it better. I have yet to run across anyone who rejects the opportunity to make their work more enjoyable and fulfilling. Remember that you are embarking on a forever journey—there is no end, just better.

Change is inevitable in organizations, and it will be hard. But change doesn't have to be lonely or uncontrolled. The Change Questions, rooted in Lean thinking and human behavioral psychology, make Change Initiatives inspiring and manageable. What better way to demonstrate to your people who get the work done, day in and day out, that you value them, respect them, and want them to be fulfilled? They will give your teams just what they need to realize their full potential.

LANCE FRITZ

Chairman, President, and Chief Executive Officer, Union Pacific Railroad
February 2023, Omaha, NE

CHANGE QUESTIONS

"Change" indicates desired future conditions. We might also call it progress. We must always ask, where are we and what are we changing toward?

As you use the methods in this book, avoid the trap of thinking of this or any approach to organizational change as a highly sequential process that moves from one stage to the next in a rigid and unrelenting order. In fact, each element overlaps with the others and will shift back and forth in terms of accomplishment and even sequence of initiation.

However, for convenience in explaining (not to mention that many individuals absorb new information better through sequenced and more structured approaches), we will go through the process in what you might think of as an idealized sequence.

The Change Initiative at Union Pacific (UP) presented here is a complex one. The change you wish to bring about may be of a simpler nature, and you may move through the Change Questions very quickly—perhaps even in a day, choosing only the ones that are appropriate for your initiative. Or your Change Initiative may be even more complex than that of UP. The beauty of the Change Questions method is that you will end up with your own customized approach to change for your organization. Please don't make this process more complex than the situation requires!

THE CHANGE QUESTIONS

What is your value-driven purpose?
- What is the situational problem you want to solve with this Change Initiative?
- What value will the Change Initiative deliver?

What is the work to be done to achieve the purpose or to solve the problem?
- What work changes are required to achieve the objectives of the Change Initiative?
- Where/how will you conduct learning trials to try out the Change Initiative in advance of the full launch?
- How will you get feedback on the Change Initiative to determine whether it's delivering the value that you expected?

How will you engage and develop employees?
- What tools, resources, and development are necessary for employees to have the capability to implement the Change Initiative?
- What is your communication plan to provide information consistently and proactively to employees/stakeholders about the Change Initiative?
- How will you provide positive recognition that will support the Change Initiative?

How will you establish a supportive management system with the appropriate leader behaviors?
- Does the existing management system support the Change Initiative?
  - If not, what changes can you propose?
- How can leaders demonstrate active and visible support of the Change Initiative?

What are your organization's beliefs, values, norms, attitudes and assumptions?
- Is your organization's culture supportive of the Change Initiative?
  - What actions can you take?

Figure 0.1: The Change Questions

THE ITERATIVE IMPLEMENTATION QUESTIONS

Once you've defined the needed change, you will:

Create and manage an Iterative Implementation Plan

- How can you best implement the Change Initiative with iterative loops for feedback and improvement?

Support and improve your Change Initiative

- How will you gain employee/stakeholder feedback and ownership of the Change Initiative?
- How will you improve the Change Initiative?

Intentional Change is Not for the Faint of Heart

M any people make New Year's resolutions. We save up all year for the one thing that we really want to change and on January 1, proudly declare the new resolution. Yet, just four weeks later, one-third of the people who made resolutions have given up on them. Ultimately, only about 12 percent of people who make an annual resolution are successful in keeping the resolution for the full year.

The cynic may say that it makes sense that the failure rate is so high because people make "big-deal" resolutions such as changing lifelong habits. Of course, these resolutions would be difficult to change, much less sustain for a full year.

OK – then what about a short-term goal such as drinking more water each day? This seems like a fairly easy thing to change as drinkable water is plentiful in many countries and doesn't require a dedicated time commitment, since most of us can drink water and do other things at the same time. According to the National Library of Medicine, it is estimated that 75 percent of American adults are chronically dehydrated. It's not like dehydration isn't important as it's a frequent cause of hospital admissions and makes many existing medical conditions worse. Solution: drink more water every day … so easy!

If it were so easy there would probably not be multiple apps available to help us make this "easy" change in our lives. These apps boast such bells and whistles as pop-up reminders, "reward" graphics for positive reinforcement, "you-messed-up" graphics when the goal is missed, hydration challenges and games to set up with others, and tracking charts and graphs, Oh ... that didn't work? How about a water bottle that infuses various flavors? No? What about a tracker placed on any water bottle that gives sip-by-sip feedback on water performance or a big, fillable bottle with markings on the side that show how much water should have been consumed by a certain time each day? For a few more dollars invested in this daily change, there is a wearable device that tracks actual hydration levels in real time. Still, with all of that, 75 percent of American adults are chronically dehydrated and are chronically saying, "I should drink more water."

Most people have examples from their personal lives that demonstrate that change is just plain hard, whether it's long-term goals that are focused on for a full year, or short-term goals, made the night before. This isn't a new concept. You may remember reading the book *The Prince* in high school or college. If not, you have probably heard of the term "Machiavellian" which is often used to describe someone who is a conniving opportunist. *The Prince* was written by Niccolo Machiavelli who lived from 1469-1527. It became one of the first leadership self-help books to be copied multiple times in multiple languages to advise European monarchies on how to be successful in leading their countries. Machiavelli spent a bit of time in *The Prince* discussing the initiation of change, which he called "a new system":

> "It must be remembered that there is nothing more difficult to plan, more doubtful of success, nor more dangerous to manage than a new system. For the initiator has the enmity of all who would profit by the preservation of the old institution and merely lukewarm defenders in those who gain by the new ones."

Machiavelli covers several key concepts here:

- "There is nothing more difficult to plan ... " Get this — 500 years ago there was recognition that a Change Initiative needed to have a plan, and it would be exceedingly difficult to create one!

- "... more doubtful of success ..." Machiavelli declared that the change would probably not succeed, even without the knowledge of the current studies, many of which place the average Change Initiative sustainment rate at 30-50 percent.

- ".... nor more dangerous to manage." There was a recognition that the Change Initiative could not be simply "rolled out." It had to be managed and managing change could be dangerous.

- "For the initiator has the enmity of all who would profit by the preservation of the old institution." Machiavelli knew that every process in an organization had people who benefited from the existing process, and if the process changed these people would not be happy.

- "... merely lukewarm defenders in those who gain by the new ones." In other words, Machiavelli didn't expect hearty support for the change, even from those who would benefit from the change.

Given all of this, one would think that Machiavelli was recommending that leaders do not deploy a new system—or new way of doing things. However, he determined that to be a successful leader, a leader must engage in *personal* change as well as *organizational* change:

"Whosoever desires constant success must change his conduct with the times."

"I'm not interested in preserving the status quo; I want to overthrow it."

Disclaimer: This discussion of Machiavelli is not intended to advocate practices he was famous for such as lying, cheating, and destroying any-thing and anyone in his path to achieve his aims. Invoking Machiavelli is useful only to demonstrate that while he clearly promoted self-interest at all costs, he was a leader who recognized that change—personal and organizational—was necessary, difficult, and beneficial.

Enough about Machiavelli. In this book, we use this working definition of a Change Initiative:

> *"An organizational Change Initiative consists of strategies and actions used to create a new method, process, structure, or culture to achieve improvement in output or performance."*

For this book, the change we'll be talking about can range from small-scale to large-scale.

Step back for a moment and think about the Change Initiatives you have been a part of. Generally, the possibility of failure is rarely, if ever, mentioned. It's almost as if the initiative will be jinxed if failure is discussed. Leaders charge forward and attempt to implement the change with a positive, can-do attitude without acknowledging that the odds are stacked against its success.

We're not advocating that you take a negative, "it-will-fail" attitude; instead, we suggest a clear-eyed acknowledgment that failure is a real threat. Anyone enacting change must proactively take steps to navigate the myriad obstacles and mitigate the risk of failure.

Our goal with the Change Questions? We want to help you to achieve the change desired and needed by you and your organization. In essence, the questions are used to help you clarify fundamental *thinking* leading to situational approaches to make targeted changes—changes that make a difference to your team and your business.

*F*or most of my life, I loved to eat sugar—anything containing sugar—you name it. Over the years, instead of feeling guilty about my sugar habit, I felt an undeserved sense of pride that I had gotten away with eating so much sugar. That is until a few years ago when my blood test pronounced me as pre-diabetic. What a wake-up call.

After getting used to the idea that I would have to change my eating habits, I decided this would be no problem whatsoever. You see, I have been leading organizational change for most of my career. Please—if anyone knows about change, I know about change.

Yeah, right. What you realized as soon as you read this, and it took a while for me to figure out, is that talking about personal change, knowing about change, and wanting to change are all vastly different from actually changing. Change is hard! Despite a visit to a dietitian, I seemed to lack the willpower to change for any sustained period. After a whole lot of research, and lots of fits and starts, I can now say that I am sustaining a new and healthy way of eating and am no longer pre-diabetic.

Why did I tell you that personal and embarrassing story about myself? Because it illustrates that individual change is extremely difficult. It is difficult even when we know and accept that the change is much needed and will be a great improvement over not changing. Therefore, how much more difficult is adoption and sustainment of organizational change when it is dependent upon individuals who don't have a vested interest or a desire to change?

Back in 2000 I was working in France and Germany and was responsible for helping our fifteen automotive fastener plants implement Lean Manufacturing. As an American woman working in these two countries, I was not very successful. I wasn't sure if the problem was my nationality, my gender, my methods, my personality, or … all the above. I started reading every article I could find about effective change management. Around that same time, I ran across a Harvard Business Review article called, "Cracking the Code of

Change," by Nitin Nohria and Michael Beer. The first sentence was, "Here's the brutal fact: 70 percent of all change initiatives fail." At that point, I considered myself lucky to hit the 30 percent sustainment rate. I decided to figure out how to buck the trend.

Every time I failed, I sought out research on how to enhance sustainment and acceptance of the Change Initiative. One failure after another helped me to develop tools and techniques that steadily increased the sustainment of the change I led from under 30 percent to over 90 percent. This book represents my attempt to share what I've learned about change with other people who are passionate about change. People, like you, who believe that change is possible and understand that change is extremely challenging in a large, complex organization … or perhaps any organization made up of human beings!

I will also share the story of the actual application of the Change Questions framework at Union Pacific. But before we get to that, let's hear my friend John Shook's change story. Throughout this book, John will share his thoughts on each step through the questions, which I hope will give you an even deeper understanding of them as well as what we were really up to at UP. We'll call these interludes John's Notes, and I hope they prompt you to take a step back and take your own mental notes as well.

---

* In subsequent years, the 70 percent failure rate has come under scrutiny. Some of the concerns with this failure rate are that (1) the studies fail to provide a solid definition of what, exactly counts as "failure," (2) the research that identifies the 70 percent rate may be anecdotal or based on faulty research, and (3) the percentage may vary according to industry type.

It is often said that "people don't like change." It's true that we don't like change that is "done to us." Effectively changing an established, complex organization is among the most difficult of all human undertakings. Far more difficult than rocket science.

My entire career has entailed bringing change to organizations. The same conundrum that bedeviled Lynn Kelley in 2000—leading her to discover the Nohria and Beer finding that 70 percent of Change Initiatives fail—led me and others in the Lean Global Network, a confederation of non-profit institutes in over thirty countries, to ask *why*—why do organizations struggle so?

Colleagues and I studied transformation failures and successes we had witnessed over the years. Investigating transformation attempts and looking for common failure modes and key success factors led us to identify what we first called the Lean Transformation Model. Observing the all-too-common phenomenon of practitioners leaping to prescriptive solutions in the form of a rigid set of steps to follow, we quickly changed the word "model" (which may have implied a fixed-step approach) to "framework." But, whatever nomenclature we may choose, transformation efforts (or Change Initiatives of any scale) that try to apply practices and even questions and principles in a prescriptive, check-the-box fashion, without individuals taking ownership *based on an understanding of what improvements they are instituting and why,* is not only disrespectful of the people who are impacted but will struggle to take root and eventually falter.

What we have found does make a difference for change leaders is an unrelenting focus on *questioning* accompanied by *fundamental thinking about how to address those questions.* Beginning by addressing questions, heuristically and situationally, can be an effective antidote to the human tendency to jump to solutions. Importantly, while the Change Questions themselves, as presented in this book and as

Lynn applied at Union Pacific and elsewhere, are critical, equally critical is the fundamental *thinking* one applies when addressing the questions. This, the fundamental thinking and situational application, is where *Lean Thinking and Practice* come into play.

So where do we start? With where we began as an organization: our value-driven purpose. Every organization had one when it started, and every individual in every organization should have one today. All should flow from there, every action by every contributor.

More about purpose soon – for now, back to Lynn.

Over many years in many organizations, John and I independently encountered similar challenges, resistance, barriers, opportunities, and tremendous potential, that invariably accompany organizational progress. And we imagine you have encountered  *them as well. The common challenges led us to respond independently, in methodical ways that unearthed common patterns, including the Change Questions and some of the methods that make up this book.*

I named my change methodology The Change Playbook. As John said, the methodology he and his colleagues use has become known globally as the Lean Transformation Framework. This book combines my playbook with the transformation framework resulting in an integrated methodology we call the **Change Questions.** *We'll get into the questions in detail later.*

First, I want to start by sharing a powerful story of change at Union Pacific Railroad, the company where I was in a leadership position for eight years, serving as vice president of continuous improvement for five years and senior vice president of supply chain and continuous improvement for three. It's easier—and certainly more interesting!— to hear a real story of change as a way of learning a new change methodology than it is to try to digest change theory. I will use UP as an example to illustrate key points about the Change Questions.

Intentional Change at the UP Railroad

The Change Questions have been used in many organizations for many types of changes. UP used them to implement its own organizational transformation. In this book, I use the story of what unfolded at UP between 2010 to 2018 to explore change in a complex organization. As you will see in the following metrics, UP was very successful, but to its lasting credit, the leadership of UP asked itself (as every successful organization should), "How can we improve employee engagement, customer satisfaction, safety performance, and operating results?"

UP's big "why"—improve employee engagement, customer satisfaction, safety performance, and operating results.

UP was designated by Abraham Lincoln over 150 years ago to unite (Union) the country from the east to the west (Pacific) while the north and the south were divided by the Civil War—thus the name, "Union Pacific."

In 2010, the vision of UP was: **Building America.** The mission statement was:

MISSION

The Men and Women of Union Pacific Are Dedicated to Serve

Union Pacific works for the good of our customers, shareholders, communities, and one another. Our commitment defines us and drives the economic strength of our company and our country.

The organizational structure of UP's Operating Department in 2010 looked like this:

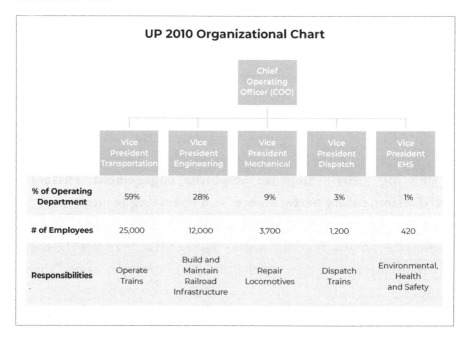

Figure 1.1: UP 2010 Operating Department Organizational Chart

UP's rail network covered twenty-three states in the western two-thirds of the US and operated over 32,000 track miles. The company provided freight transportation in areas such as agricultural products, automotive, chemicals, energy, industrial products, and intermodal. UP connected with other rail carriers to move freight across North America and Mexico. Its annual revenue was $16.1 billion, and it was 164 on the *Fortune* 500 list. In 2010, there were 48,000 employees with 42,000 employees in the Operating Department.

At UP, the Change Initiative highlighted in this book came to be called the UP Way. For us, it was a form of Lean Management or Lean Thinking and Practice. For those of you who are not familiar with Lean, it is a widely used approach with origins in systems and methods of Toyota

Motor Corporation to attain better performance through engaging employees in streamlining operations and improving customer satisfaction. The definition of Lean that we'll use in this book comes from the Lean Enterprise Institute:

> *"Lean is a way of thinking about creating needed value with fewer resources and less waste. Lean is a practice consisting of continuous experimentation to achieve perfect value with zero waste. Lean thinking and practice occur together."*

*B*efore joining UP Railroad, I worked at Textron for twelve years, implementing wide-scale change in thirty-two different countries and across an employee base of 35,000. By this time, the Change Questions process had gone through multiple revisions and was delivering high levels of change sustainability in areas as diverse as engineering, human resources, manufacturing, finance, and supply chain.

One day I received a voice message at my Textron office, which turned out to be from a recruiter. The gentleman said, "We would like for you to call us regarding a job which is similar to the position you now have now with Textron but instead of running an existing continuous improvement (CI) program, you will design the CI approach, implement it, and subsequently run it." I had never returned a recruiter's call before, but I was intrigued.

The job was vice president of continuous improvement for UP Railroad, headquartered in Omaha, Nebraska. During the first interview, I was told that it would involve launching the CI methodology called Lean to the Operating Department consisting of over 42,000 employees. During my next interview with the CEO and the COO, I said, "If you want to go fast, fast, fast, I'm not your person. If you want to do this without thinking about employee engagement, I'm not your person. I believe in strategic *speed—which means that we would probably have several learning trials to create buy-in, we would implement progress checks so that we can adjust as needed before full implementation, and the timeline would be modified as needed in the beginning until we refine the approach—but once we implement, it will sustain." I remember both the CEO and the COO said, "That's what we want also."*

In contrast to my position at Textron, where I was responsible for implementing multiple types of change across many different departments and functions in the company, the role at UP was very specific. I was hired to implement continuous improvement using Lean principles across the Operating Department, encompassing employees within twenty-three states. For the most part, many of the employees who would be involved in our Lean activities only rarely interacted with a supervisor, and even more rarely were under one roof, as they were doing jobs on the railroad such as running trains and repairing track.

We are often told that change adoption is most successful when there is a "burning platform," also known as an imminent and urgent need to change. Some change methodologies promote this concept so strongly that they even encourage creating a crisis or urgency if none exists, to motivate people to change. I quickly found that there was no crisis at UP. In fact, in 2010, when I started at UP, the company was doing well. It had recovered from the Great Recession before many other companies, and the biggest problem was hiring enough employees to keep up with demand.

Customer satisfaction was steadily increasing.

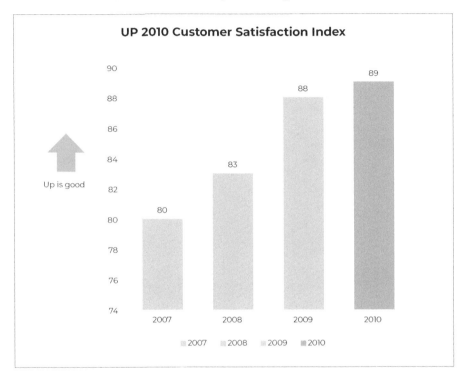

Figure 1.2: UP 2010 Customer Satisfaction Index

Employee safety, a key metric for UP was at a "best-ever" low as measured by reportable personal injury incidents.

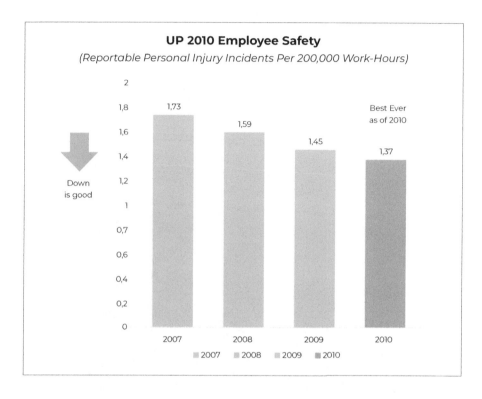

Figure 1.3: UP 2010 Employee Safety

One of the key performance indicators was velocity/service delivery, versus carload volume. The following chart shows that in 2010, UP delivered some of its highest velocity levels given the increased volume levels.

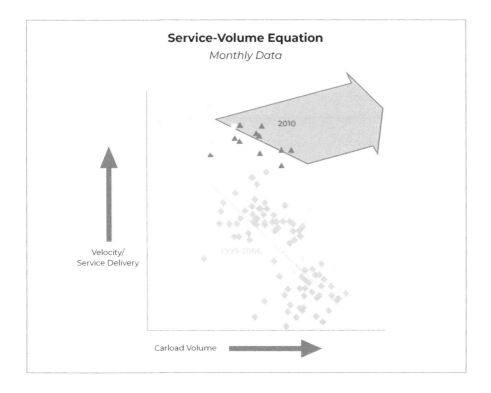

Figure 1.4: UP Service-Volume Equation Model

The drive to transform to the Lean operating system was led by the COO, Lance Fritz, who had a manufacturing background before coming to UP. He saw the power of Lean on the factory floor and felt that it would greatly benefit the railroad in operating efficiently, but equally as important to him, he felt it would build employee engagement. Approximately three months before we launched Lean in the Operating Department, we formed a planning team (called the change team) to answer the very same questions we outline in this book. We named our Lean transformation the UP Way.

I'll share more about the steps we went through at UP as we go through the Change Questions. They are intended as examples of ways to interpret each step of the change framework. You may replicate some of the solutions in the case study or may find your own answers within the change framework steps.

90+ Percent Sustainment of the UP Way

*If I were you at this point, I'd be wondering why I should trust the Change Questions to deliver results. There are many stories throughout this book to answer this question; however, one of the biggest measures that companies look for is sustainment of the activity itself. Did UP Way sustain itself in all areas of the organization? Given that in many companies, sustainment of Change Initiatives is often difficult, I want to provide you with the sustainment data, as well as information on how we calculated sustainment at UP because that, in and of itself, can be tricky. To jump to the punch line: **by the time I retired in 2018, our team's average sustainment of the multiple changes that we implemented across the railroad through UP Way was over 90 percent. We measured sustainment by tracking key sustainment/improvement metric(s) for each change for six months to one year after we fully implemented the change.***

To call the initiative "sustained," the key metric had to be at the same rate or better than what it was when the improvement was fully implemented. Improvement projects were fully implemented when the performance goal was met. We measured the rate until there were six consecutive months in the "better" range. If the Change Initiative could not produce that sustained improvement it was considered non-sustained. (Additional information about calculating the sustainment metric is included later in this book). This is just to give you some context for where UP began with its Lean transformation using the Change Questions framework. But first, a few words again from John.

Note: All references to UP are time-based from 2010 as shown in this chapter, through 2018 as shown in subsequent chapters, and may not reflect the current state. All names of UP employees referenced in this book have been changed except for Lance Fritz. This chapter identifies him as COO. In 2015, Lance was named chairman, president, and CEO.

By Lynn's account, UP was highly successful, maybe even on a roll, when they hired her. The question, then, is why? Why did UP hire Lynn Kelley as vice president of continuous improvement in 2010? Why did Lance Fritz want UP to become a Lean organization?

I have never visited UP, so it was easy for me to adopt a "beginner's mindset" and begin alongside you, the reader, by applying the Change Questions right away. And so, we address the first question of purpose or *why*—what was UP's purpose? What problem were they trying to solve? What target condition did they have in mind? What was the "job to be done" for the executive position of VP of CI?

Most of the time, we start with what is in front of us. If we are being chased by a bear, we first get out of the way—we think later about why we got ourselves in such a dangerous situation. But, indeed, the *purpose* question is never far away, especially as we get started with any intentional change. The earnest and well-read executives of UP wanted to become a Lean organization, and unlike what happens to so many Change Initiatives at other organizations, they wanted the initiative to *sustain* itself.

Entropy in physics is well understood. In organizations, entropy is little understood but widely acknowledged. Do we wait until entropy sets in before we act, or can we be proactive and preventive in our stance? Experienced executives know that hard times are just around the bend. The UP executive team, led directly by the CEO, decided to be proactive. We should all be so wise more often!

In fact, so often we speak of change as if it is a monolithic thing, a mechanical device. We ask whether the Change Initiative at a particular company was a success or failure, as if organizational dynamics were a football game. If we want lasting, sustainable success, then, if we are playing a football game it is an endless one. The score is always changing, a winning score today does not mean organizations will still be winning tomorrow. Conditions on the field are in a state of constant evolution. But organizations are less like mechanical devices and more like organisms, so it is more useful for us to think in terms of aiding the organization/organism in evolving to a sounder state rather than like fine-tuning a fine clock.

In other words, rather than proclaiming success or failure, better to get on with the work of making things better! And better to begin *now* rather than wait until we have the perfect plan and fall behind.

Introducing the Change Questions

The Change Questions proposed in this book represent natural queries with which to approach key organizational decisions. They are agnostic in they have no point of view, rather they come to life as you address them with the *fundamental thinking* – which is anything but agnostic – you can use to improve your situation. You may have already considered some of these questions as you've made decisions in the past, but here we present key questions and key principles in a methodical way to help you approach any needed change more effectively.

Figure 1.5: The Change Questions Diagram

The Change Questions represent a new way of thinking and acting characterized not by implementing a series of steps or solutions but by addressing key issues of *purpose, process, and people*. In this way, they function as an investigative process that can be used by any organization or individual to determine a situational and customized approach to change. The questions help organizations transform in desired ways while mitigating the common problem of applying a cut-and-paste change methodology to diverse situations and initiatives.

The Change Questions are listed at the front of this book and the question mark diagram in figure 1.5 shows the foundation of the Change Questions. Each section of the question mark has a dedicated chapter. The chapters include background and research on the topic, how to think about the questions that are asked within the topic, and how UP answered them.

The five simple but powerful overarching questions are continually addressed via fundamental thinking along with a complementary improvement process. The Change Questions and principles employed to address them can be used by anyone responsible for achieving any Change Initiative within your organization.

The **High Level Change Questions** that follow will guide you through designing the change. The answers to these questions will then inform your iterative implementation planning.

1 **Purpose**: *What is your value-driven purpose?*
People have a strong desire to understand why they need to change and to understand the benefit of the change whenever they are being asked to change. Some organizations skip the important step of defining and effectively communicating the purpose of the change, thereby risking aligned focus and employee engagement. It is important to gain alignment on the problem you want to solve with the initiative, and the value you expect to get from implementation of the change. Everything comes back to purpose.

2 **Design, Do, and Improve**: *What is the work to be done to achieve the purpose or to solve the problem?*

Once you define your purpose and clarify your problem(s) to be solved, you will need to determine what needs to be done to achieve it. This is enabled by having a deep understanding of the situation, including knowledge of the work at a micro level as well as the environment where the change will take place. The better you understand how the work is conducted today, the better you can design the work differently to better achieve your newly defined purpose.

3 **Engage and Develop Employees**: *How will you engage and develop employees?*

As you gain a sense of what capabilities are demanded by the new way(s) of working, you need to plan for how employees will develop or acquire those capabilities. You will also think about how to provide resources and assistance to employees doing the new work. Frequent and consistent communication is critical, as well as recognition for employees who are sucessfully accomplishing the change.

4 **Management System and Leadership**: *How will you establish a supportive management system with the appropriate leader behaviors?*

One reason often cited as a major cause of Change Initiative failure is the lack of a supportive management system and of visible leadership commitment. The Change Questions framework will help you obtain input from leadership, gain commitment to the initiative at hand, and gauge how well the management system supports it.

5 **Culture**: *What are your organization's beliefs, values, norms, attitudes, and assumptions?*

The culture of your organization, which includes (among other things) the *fundamental thinking* of all the people in it, will profoundly impact every aspect of the change and its success. Culture appears as central to the entire process in the Change Questions diagram because of its profound influence on all the other aspects of change. You will need to understand your culture, its impact, and the importance of taking it into consideration throughout the change process.

Iterative Implementation Plan: Your answers to the Change Questions will come together in the form of an iterative implementation plan. It is "iterative" because we focus not only on the implementation steps but also on the *built-in* improvement activities you will use to obtain feedback and improve your Change Initiative over time.

A characteristic of this approach versus other change methods you may have encountered is that you use the Change Questions to customize *your* Change Initiative around the needs of *your* organization. By choosing the elements that are most appropriate to your situation, and answering the corresponding questions, you ultimately increase the probability of success for your initiative.

The first time you use the Change Questions methodology you may follow them in the order given in this book. Individuals often absorb new information through sequenced and more structured approaches; however, organizations are systems, and systems are filled with complex, overlapping, and connected elements, each influencing the other. This is nowhere more evident than in the UP Railroad story that illustrates the points in each chapter. For example, you will find traces of the purpose, employee engagement, development, leadership, management system, and cultural elements within the design, do, and improve chapter. As in the case of UP, the same overlap will be true in your own journey through the Change Questions. Once you are familiar with the questions, you can use them in whatever sequence works for you.

The UP examples throughout the book demonstrate comprehensive change approaches for a complex change in a large, geographically distributed organization. If you are reading this book with a change in mind that is fairly straightforward, you may think that the UP examples are overkill. We would agree with you in *your* situation. We have provided this large-scale change example so that you might down-select, choosing only the approaches that are needed for your situation, rather than the alternative of providing a bare-bones example that leaves much to interpretation.

These questions and topics are covered in detail in chapters 2-8 and are brought together in a comprehensive summary in chapter 9 which is where we get into the process of how to make the change real. Chapter 9 includes sample agendas, deliverables, and suggested stakeholders to be involved at various stages of the process. The sample agendas correspond with the chapters in this book. We hope you will use the guide in Chapter 9 to start making the Change Questions your own so you can get to work with your team. You and your team will find fillable PDF forms in the Change Questions digital workbook by scanning the following QR code or using the link.

changequestions.net

Many organizations go straight from deciding on a change directly to implementing it. Other organizations have an idea for a change, create an action plan, and immediately go about implementing it. Both situations ignore the advance planning activities that will ensure that the change *sustains and continues to mature as the organization matures and surrounding circumstances evolve.*

Sure, it's a lot of upfront work when you may just want to get started on your Change Initiative right away—or you may have been told that you have to start right away! Still, we know that using the Change Questions and doing thoughtful planning along with checking and adjusting throughout, will save your organization enormous time, resources, and effort.

Define Purpose

Figure 2.1: Change Questions Diagram - Purpose

"*I*n all my other previous jobs, I had worked my way up in an organization, so I didn't realize the challenges of joining a company at the senior leadership level. Not only did I not know the industry, but I didn't know anyone at the company. I needed to form a team to work through the Change Questions but had to rely on choosing *people based on their roles without knowing if we could easily work together or even if they were supportive of the Change Initiative. As you will learn in this chapter, it turns out that the leadership was more aligned behind the initiative than the change team which was tasked to plan how we would introduce it to 42,000 employees. Welcome to the real world!*

In the purpose section of the Change Questions, you will reflect upon the problem you are trying to solve or the condition you want to achieve with the change. That reflection will lead you to develop a purpose statement. Think too about the value you believe you will get from the successful adoption of the Change Initiative, which you will articulate in several value statements.

Forming the Change Team

You will almost always work through the Change Questions with a team. A core team of three to five people often works well. A larger team may slow down the decision making. You will want to consider the characteristics of the people who are best suited for the team. Some common traits to look for in team members tend to be openness to new ideas, respect from peers, possession of the required expertise, and good project management skills. It is important to include subject-matter experts and employees who are going to be implementing the change (i.e., a union environment will call for union representation).

In some cases, it may be possible for an individual to work through the elements of the Change Questions, drawing in stakeholders and experts as needed or in a round-robin fashion to gather input from appropriate people.

Planning vs. Implementation

Chapters 2-6 in this book describe the work to be done in each of the steps within the Change Questions. It is important to understand that while you work your way through these chapters, you are firmly in the planning stage of your Change Initiative, rather than the implementation stage, which is covered in chapters 7-8. For example, when we discuss improving your Change Initiative, you are planning how to improve it. When we discuss employee engagement, you are planning how to engage employees. Occasionally, you will actually *do* more than plan by writing your purpose statement or developing your training material, for example, but you won't move these things forward yet. Once all these planning steps are complete, you will integrate the actual work of these steps into your iterative implementation plan and begin the launch of your change.

The answers to the Change Questions in this phase will help you to develop your purpose statement and your value statements.

Change Questions

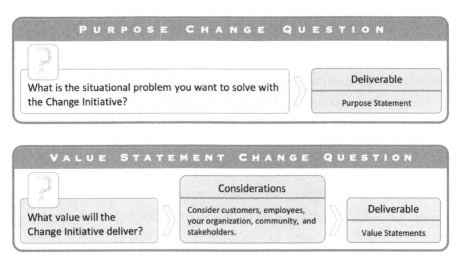

Figure 2.2: Purpose Change Questions

Writing the Purpose Statement

It seems like common sense that you would describe the Change Initiative and its purpose before launching the change. In a wide-scale study, 79 percent of business leaders said that a defined purpose was central to business success. However, only 34 percent of the same leaders felt that a defined purpose was used as a guidepost in their organization. Unfortunately, many organizations skip this important first step.

Purpose Statement Definition: A sentence that briefly describes the initiative and the outcome/reason for it. To assist the team in writing the purpose statement, you can start by answering this question:

- What situational problem are you trying to solve with this Change Initiative?

After discussing the situational problem that you and your team are trying to solve through the change, your team will write the purpose statement. There is a temptation to spend hours meticulously wordsmithing the purpose statement to include every possibility and nuance. That is not a productive use of time this early in the game. A simple sentence that everyone can agree upon is sufficient.

Many purpose statements are structured within a two-part sentence. The first part often tells WHAT the initiative is (e.g., implement a new customer service program). The second part of the sentence tells WHY (e.g., to improve customer response time). In a later step, the team will use the purpose statement to craft the vision statement. If your organization has a communications department, you can include a member from it to assist in forming the vision statement. The vision statement is sometimes time-consuming to develop; therefore, we don't recommend that you halt the momentum this early in the process by creating one now. The purpose statement will serve the need for alignment, feedback, support, and communication at this time.

Creating the Value Statements

The next step is to identify the benefit, or the value you expect to obtain once the change is implemented. We call these value statements. Organizations don't do change just for the sake of change; it's always to deliver something of value.

This will become increasingly important as you implement the Change Initiative because ultimately you will measure the actual benefit that you are getting from the change and compare it to the value you defined in your value statements. If you do not see the benefit of the change, you will need to make improvements to the initiative to obtain the expected value.

Value statement definition: a sentence that describes the expected benefit that the Change Initiative should deliver.

Many people are familiar with S.M.A.R.T goals, as proposed by George Doran. According to Doran, a goal/objective should be:

- Specific—target a specific area for improvement,
- Measurable—quantify or suggest an indicator of progress,
- Assignable—specify who will do it,
- Realistic—state what results can realistically be achieved, given available resources,
- Time-related—specify when the result(s) can be achieved.

The first two elements of S.M.A.R.T can be used in the creation of the value statements if it is helpful for the team. The remaining elements of S.M.A.R.T. may be used and defined by your team later in the change process.

Examples of specific and measurable value statements are:

- The new organizational chart will streamline the customer ordering process.

- The new warehouse management system will increase inventory accuracy.
- The new process for switching railcars will reduce yard dwell time.

Specific: target a specific area for improvement	Measurable: quantify or suggest an indicator of progress
Customer interface as identified in the organizational chart	Streamline (reduce the number of steps for customers) in the ordering process
Warehouse management system	Increase inventory accuracy
Railcar switching process	Reduce yard dwell time

Figure 2.3: Specific and Measurable Examples

At this early stage, you may not be able to quantify or set a numerical goal for measurable improvement. You are simply identifying which specific areas you will measure. Keep in mind that whatever you determine for the value statement will be measured by your team once the initiative is implemented. So, if you don't have an existing measurement tool in place, you will develop one in a future step within the Change Questions.

The number of value statements generally ranges from one to five. Non-complex Change Initiatives generally require fewer value statements than complex ones. Some of the initiatives we've led have had only one or two value statements.

Leadership Buy-In

The purpose statement and associated value statements need to express the thinking of top leadership involved in the change. In a later step, we will include a broader level of leadership in Change Initiative activities. This initial engagement is ordinarily completed with a small number of top leader(s) who have a desire for the change. As a change team leader, you may find that once you define the change and gain feedback from the top leader(s), the purpose statement or value statements may change, or the need for the change is revised. It is better to know this now rather than later in the game.

Sometimes a leader has not requested a change, but the work team has determined a change is necessary and it cannot be implemented without leadership agreement. In this scenario, this purpose step is even more critical, as you and your team will use the purpose statement to gain the perspectives and engagement of leadership before moving forward.

Aligning the Change Team

Since the success or failure of any change is largely a function of alignment around the purpose or desirability of the change, it is imperative that the members of the change team are aligned. Alignment cannot always be assumed, especially since your change team may include representatives from many areas of the organization, some of which may not even be supportive of the change. Successful teams have team leaders who take the responsibility to understand the thinking of the team members and facilitate conversations to get these players aligned. Depending on the degree of cohesion upfront, this work may (and probably will) entail many different actions, such as asking for opinions, calling on people who tend to be quiet during meetings, and encouraging active dialogue to work out disagreements in a respectful manner.

If you find that the team is not at all aligned, or you can't tell if the team is aligned because people are not willing to speak up (which is a serious problem in its own right), there are several helpful tools you can use. The G.R.P.I. model of team effectiveness has been in use for many years. The acronym stands for Goals, Roles, Process, and Interpersonal. These are four areas that Richard Beckhard found to be key for well-functioning teams.

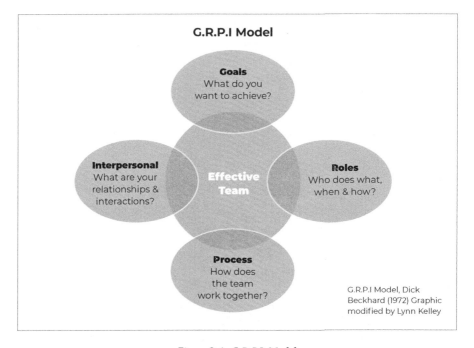

Figure 2.4: G.R.P.I. Model

You can use this framework or another method of your choosing to gather feedback on how well the team is functioning. We have used the G.R.P.I. tool as follows:

1. Ask the team for feedback around each of the G.R.P.I. questions.
   a. Sample questions can be found online, or you can write your own that cover each of these four topics.
   b. Send a survey to each team member after the first meeting with the opportunity to respond anonymously if there is a low trust level.

2. At the next team meeting, display the individual scores for each question in a graph format that shows the differences between members. If you are concerned about mistrust within the team, you can display the scores without identifying team members. The

following example shows an abbreviated G.R.P.I. format; there are usually several questions asked for each of the four categories.

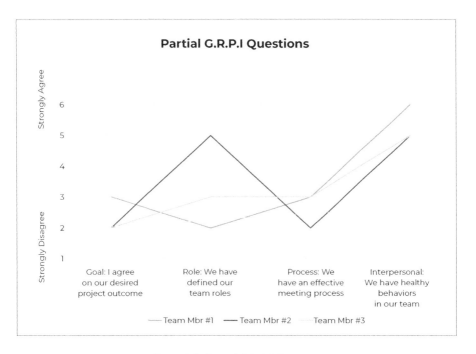

Figure 2.5: Partial G.R.P.I. Questions

3. At your next team meeting, discuss each of the G.R.P.I questions that show nonalignment. Evaluation of this situation shows:
    a. Goal: The three team members primarily feel that they do NOT agree on the desired project outcome.
    b. Role: Two of the team members don't feel that the roles are defined, but team member two feels that the roles are defined.
    c. Process: The three team members primarily feel that the team does not have an effective meeting process.
    d. Interpersonal: The good news is that all three of the team members agree that they have healthy interpersonal behaviors in the team.

4. After discussing the items and determining actions, the team leader may administer the survey after each meeting until the team shows alignment.

PURPOSE—HOW TO DO IT

Purpose Statement and Value Statements

The first Question to be answered by the UP change team was:

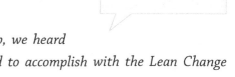

- *What is the situational problem that we need to address?*

In our interviews with leadership, we heard themes regarding what they wanted to accomplish with the Lean Change Initiative:

- *Involve employees in making things better within their workplace,*
- *Improve customer service, and*
- *Increase employee engagement.*

At this point in the process, we recognized that we did not have a name for the Lean approach at UP. Several years prior, the Mechanical Department had begun implementing Lean. We decided to initially adopt the name, UP Way, as a working title to be confirmed or changed as we proceeded through the planning stages. And by reflecting upon the "problems we were trying to solve," we developed a one-sentence purpose statement that defined UP Way and reflected several reasons for implementing the initiative:

UP Way Purpose Statement

The UP Way will be deployed in the Operating Department and will engage employees in improving the way they work.

The value statements for UP Way were an expansion of the information we had gathered from our discussions with leadership, employees, and stakeholders regarding the proposed initiative. We created "specific" and "measurable" columns to help us define the value statements using the first two aspects of the S.M.A.R.T. methodology.

Specific: target a specific area for improvement	Measurable: quantify or suggest an indicator of progress
Empowered employees	Improve customer service
UP Way application to safety activities and operations in the field	Improve safety and operational performance
Skilled employees	Increase utilization of UP Way tools
Train employees in problem solving	Build a problem solving culture
Employee involvement in UP Way	Increase employee engagement

Figure 2.6: UP's Specific and Measurable Example

UP Way Value Statements

1. Empowered employees are improving customer service.
2. UP Way activities in the field improve safety and operational performance.
3. Employees are skilled in UP Way concepts and are using them in the workplace.
4. Training people in UP Way problem solving tools is building a problem solving culture (Problem Solving is one of the five elements of the UP Way as illustrated on page 126).
5. Employee involvement in UP Way increases employee engagement.

After we completed the work in this section, we scheduled a meeting with the top leadership at UP to review the purpose statement and the value statements. Leadership was in agreement with the work we had done with only a few minor changes that involved wording and not substance.

Immediately following this meeting, I sent each member the G.R.P.I. survey, reminding them to keep in mind the goals, roles, processes, and interpersonal aspects of the work. I asked the change team members to return the G.R.P.I. survey within two days (it took approximately five minutes to complete). I used an online survey tool to make the survey anonymous. I was concerned about the alignment of the team for several reasons. I was new to UP and didn't have existing relationships and trust with the team members. The team members were from different departments within UP and had taken on the change team membership in addition to their work tasks. Many of them were short on time, energy, and engagement in the initiative. I also sensed that many of the people on the change team viewed UP Way as a "flavor of the month," which would quickly disappear as the company moved on to the next shiny initiative. My impression was that they didn't think the UP Way would last and would be a waste of their time.

When the first set of G.R.P.I. survey responses was returned, it was as I suspected. The team was not aligned on most of the items. I presented the results to the team. Since the survey was anonymous, we did not know who said what. We discussed each area and decided upon what we could do as a team to improve our alignment. I did not ask people to identify their answers, I simply asked them to think of ways that we could improve each item. This was a safe environment for people to make suggestions. For example, "We have defined team roles" received a low score. I thought that since the change team members were representing the departments they came from, they understood their roles as department representatives. That was not the case, so we decided as a group that each person's role would be defined as the following:

1. Keeping their department leadership and stakeholders informed on the team's work through weekly updates,

2. Getting feedback from their department leadership and stakeholders to bring back to the change team,

3. Taking on assignments within the change team, and

4. Contributing actively during the meetings.

The next week when we did the G.R.P.I. survey, the responses showed that this item was no longer a problem.

Practical Application: Purpose

When we started implementing UP Way in the Harriman Dispatch Center, we had strong support from Raymond, who was responsible for the Harriman operations. The building itself is a wonderfully historic brick structure that deceptively holds state-of-the-art digital capabilities that dictate the movement of every train on the system. The interior walls of the building and each workstation are filled with screens that contain blinking lights of multiple colors indicating the movement of all of the trains on UP's 32,000 miles of track.

Those 32,000 track miles are divided into twenty-two service units, each one connecting with adjacent service units. Now comes the tricky part—while individual train dispatchers direct train movements within discreet territories, the actual on-the-ground movement of the physical train is the responsibility of a director in the field. There are 22 directors of train management (DTMs) located in the Harriman Dispatch Center and twenty-two directors of transportation service (DTSs) located in the field. Each DTM-DTS pair is responsible for their performance metrics within the same geographic location, and of course, each of them has an impact on the other's performance metrics—which does not always lead to the easiest of partnerships.

Raymond decided to use UP Way at Harriman to increase train velocity. Each of the 22 DTMs started UP Way activities to address the challenges in their service unit. Results started coming in and garnered the attention of Raymond's boss, Ebony, who said, "Wait a minute – the DTMs can't do this on their own, they need to partner with the DTSs." Meanwhile, the DTSs were busy on their service units and working on velocity. In some cases, the activities of the DTMs were optimizing the Harriman metrics at the expense of the field metrics and vice versa.

Once the DTM-DTS pairs united around the cooperative purpose of increasing velocity, the results were dramatic. Not only did velocity increase, but associated metrics such as the recrew rate (which is caused when crews prematurely "time-out" on a delayed train) also improved.

One example of a game-changing solution that DTM-DTS pairs jointly discovered was around the speed limits which designated the maximum authorized speed for different categories of trains at any given location. The speed limits were determined by things like the track components, curvature of the track, steepness of the grade, and distance to the next signal. Since most of these elements don't change often, few people questioned the speed limits. That was the case until one DTS-DTM pair began digging more deeply into what was slowing down trains. They realized that some of those track characteristics had changed over the 150 years that UP had been in existence, but no one had bothered to update the speed limits. The DTM-DTS pair found, for example, that curves had been straightened somewhat and grade crossings had been eliminated with a bridge, allowing the speed limit to be raised.

Once each DTS-DTM pair started questioning every speed restriction they were surprised to discover how often they could raise the speed limits. Since trains neither slow down nor accelerate quickly the improvements were enormous in terms of velocity, fuel, crew costs, and customer service.

Significant intentional change rarely occurs from the efforts of one individual. It takes a team. We know this. But teams do not necessarily form easily or immediately. The same intentionality required of the entire effort is required for forming your team. And that requires true alignment around purpose.

John's **N O T E S**

Even choosing *who* will be on your team is a function of purpose. A change in enterprise purpose is a matter for the most senior executives and ownership. But even a relatively minor change, say, creating a new recruiting perk to attract the right applicants, demands having the right people on the team. Determining the right people and aligning them to the task are questions of articulating purpose.

> **"Purpose – not strategy – is the reason an organization exists. Its definition and articulation must be top management's first responsibility."**
>
> CHRISTOPHER A. BARTLETT AND SUMANTRA GHOSHAL, *HARVARD BUSINESS REVIEW*

We can use various questions to address purpose. What is our "True North?" In other words, what statement can guide us?

Harvard innovation pioneer Clayton Christensen argued for the value of articulating the "job to be done" for any product or service. Rather than draw attention to "problems"—which can be seen as a negative force—positive inquiry promotes focusing on what works well and asks questions such as, "What is our target condition?" to align and tap into a team's positive energy. In observing many organization leaders wrestle with this elusive subject matter and the terminology to address it, I have found the simple question, "What problem do we need to address?" to be highly effective in most circumstances. It can draw out matters that are deep and broad and fundamental to the organization. Steve Jobs reportedly liked to ask, "What problem will this product solve for the customer?" as well as problems that are as micro as you can imagine, such as the telling example above when Raymond recognized that the Harriman Dispatch Center needed to increase train velocity.

From there, with alignment around the problem to solve, a team can be off and running. It sounds simple, and it is. But simple doesn't mean easy, and this most basic issue trips up more teams than any issue I find. It is always worth taking the time to clarify your team's purpose/problem and revisit it from time to time.

Summary

In this section, we discussed the formation of the change team and the need for this team to be truly aligned. The team's first task, ideally completed at the first meeting, is to create a purpose statement and value statements. We strongly recommend that you make sure leadership has input into both items to gain their full commitment to the purpose and the value of your Change Initiative.

If you want to begin working on the Change Questions right away, at this point in each chapter we will refer you to the guide in chapter 9 and the digital workbook accessed through the link/QR code provided. For your convenience, in this chapter only, we have provided a sample of what you can find in the guide and the workbook.

Agenda

Here is a sample agenda for the purpose element of the Change Questions approach.

Agenda: Purpose

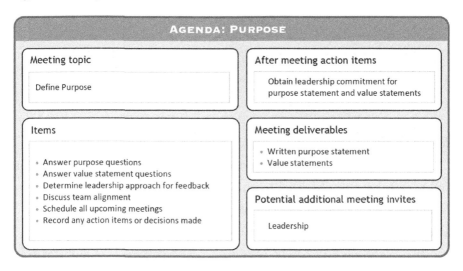

Figure 2.7: Purpose Meeting Agenda

Purpose Change Questions

Your change team will answer the following Purpose questions.

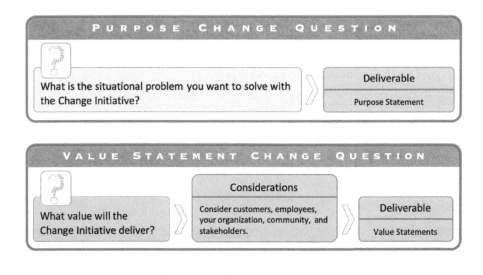

Figure 2.8: Purpose Change Questions

The digital workbook

You will have access to the digital workbook which contains the forms and tables that were highlighted in the chapter in a fillable PDF format. You can save this digital file and use it as a living document to record your team's work and track progress. Use the following link or QR code to access the digital workbook.

changequestions.net

Purpose section of the digital workbook

PURPOSE

What is the situational problem you want to solve with this Change Initiative?

GOAL: Ensures that your team and leadership have an understanding of the purpose of the Change Initiative and the expected value you believe you will get from it.

INSTRUCTIONS: Answer each Change Question below, indicated by the symbol

For additional instructions in completing this section, refer to the *Change Questions* book: **Chapter 2**

Many purpose statements are structured within a two-part sentence.

The first part tells WHAT the Change Initiative is.

UP Way Example

Purpose Statement Example:

UP Way will be deployed in the Operating department, which will engage employees in improving the way they work.

The second part of the sentence tells WHY.

Write Purpose Statement Here:

What value will the Change Initiative deliver?

INSTRUCTIONS: Complete the table below. The number of value statements generally range from 1-5.

CONSIDERATIONS: Common areas of value are delivered to: customers, employees, organization, community, and stakeholders.

DEFINITION:

| Value Statement | A sentence that describes the expected benefit that the Change Initiative should deliver. |

Specific: The first part targets a specific area for improvement.

Measurable: The second part provides a measurable indicator of progress.

Value statement: Combine the specific area for improvement and the measurable indicator of progress to make a cohesive sentence.

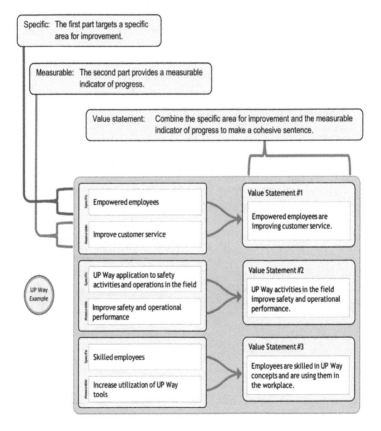

Empowered employees

Improve customer service

Value Statement #1
Empowered employees are improving customer service.

UP Way application to safety activities and operations in the field

Improve safety and operational performance

Value Statement #2
UP Way activities in the field improve safety and operational performance.

Skilled employees

Increase utilization of UP Way tools

Value Statement #3
Employees are skilled in UP Way concepts and are using them in the workplace.

UP Way Example

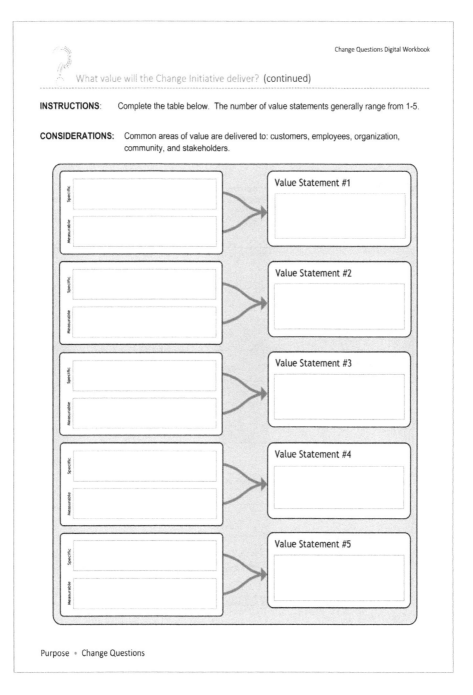

What value will the Change Initiative deliver? (continued)

INSTRUCTIONS: Complete the table below. The number of value statements generally range from 1-5.

CONSIDERATIONS: Common areas of value are delivered to: customers, employees, organization, community, and stakeholders.

Value Statement #1

Value Statement #2

Value Statement #3

Value Statement #4

Value Statement #5

Purpose • Change Questions

Figure 2.9: Purpose section of The Digital Workbook

DECISIONS

GOAL: To capture all decisions made related to the Change Initiative, both inside the team and by others outside of the team. This memorializes the decisions and prevents unnecessary revisitation of decisions.

INSTRUCTIONS: Whenever the team makes a decision related to the Change Initiative, record it on this form. For additional instructions in completing this section, refer to the *Change Questions* book.

	Decision:	Decided By:	Date:
1			
2			
3			
4			
5			
6			
7			
8			
9			
10			

Figure 2.10: Decisions section of the digital workbook

TEAM ACTION ITEMS

GOAL: To ensure deliverables related to the Change Initiative are captured and tracked until completion. The team action items are used for the pre-work involved in the Change Initiative.

INSTRUCTIONS: Revisit this working document at the end of each team meeting. Review the items that have been completed and update the document. Add all new items, and agree upon who will do each one, by when. As you work through some of the other worksheets, deliverables will naturally occur and can be placed here. For additional instructions in completing this section, refer to *Change Questions* book.

	Deliverable(s)	Owner	Target Date	Date Completed	Notes
1					
2					
3					
4					
5					
6					
7					
8					
9					
10					

Figure 2.11: Team action items section of the digital workbook

Design, Do, and Improve the Work

—

Figure 3.1: Change Questions Diagram - Design, Do, and Improve

*E*ven though I joined UP with the task of implementing Lean, it was my understanding that the actual design of UP's Lean approach was not defined—which, to me, was one of the exciting things about the job. I couldn't wait to start thinking about

Lynn's
STORY

how I would introduce Lean to UP. However, it was clear to me that I needed to better understand the organization before the team and I "designed the work." Thank goodness I didn't just dive in without understanding the organization. You will see shortly that there were several surprises, some personal disappointments, but overall ... progress.

W e all know that while change comes at us relentlessly, like it or not, a formal *Change Initiative* as an intentional activity doesn't happen on its own. The value of any change is ultimately only obtained through changes to the actual work that is done. New work or changes to existing work should be designed with that understanding in mind.

So, it is important to *try out* any new work as *part of the design process* to help assure that the change delivers the desired outcome(s). Even then, you can't assume that the change will automatically deliver value, so as you measure it, you will need to continue to improve the work to be done, checking and adjusting along the way as you assess whether the new work is delivering the value you expect. In this chapter, we discuss designing the work involved in your change, how the work will be done, and how to improve it.

You may already be familiar with the Plan, Do, Check, Act cycle, also known as PDCA (or PDSA for Plan, Do, Study, Act). The PDCA cycle is based on the scientific method and has been adopted by many organizations as a standardized way to conceptualize and actualize improvement. In addition to applying to any ongoing work of any enterprise, PDCA can also be applied to the design and introduction of an *initiative itself.* In this chapter, we will follow the PDCA cycle as it is applied to *design, do, and improve* a formal Change Initiative, while continuing to explore the example at UP.

PDCA is an iterative improvement cycle as follows:

- Plan: propose a change in a process, based on a thorough grasp of initial conditions,
- Do: implement the change or try it out,
- Check (or study): measure and analyze the results,
- Act: take appropriate action such as adjusting, standardizing, or abandoning the activity.

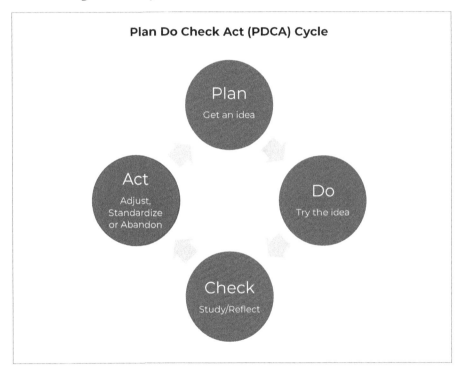

Figure 3.2: Plan Do Check Act (PDCA) Cycle

You can see in the following diagram how the design, do, and improve elements of the Change Questions integrate into the PDCA cycle. Each element of the cycle will be discussed in detail throughout this chapter.

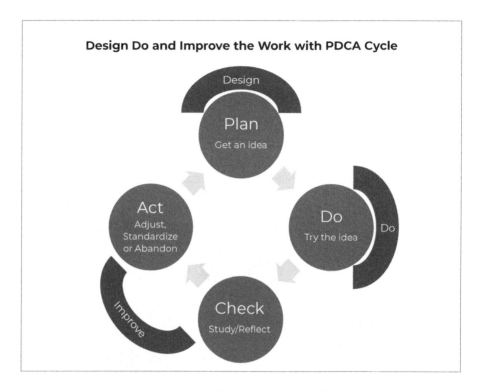

Figure 3.3: Design, Do, and Improve the Work with PDCA Cycle

Change Question

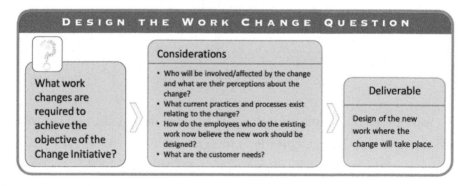

Figure 3.4: Design the Work Change Question

If you are going to lead a Change Initiative, you will probably find one of the following situations:

1. The design of the work of the initiative is defined.
2. The design of the work of the initiative is undefined.

Defined

Your change team may be given a solution to implement which already has a well-defined plan for how the work is to be done. This plan may include work instructions and other methods that assist employees in carrying out the new way of doing things. If this is the case, your goal in the design/plan step is to validate that the planned design is appropriate. We suggest using whatever methods make sense to do so and you can also use the tools outlined in the next section to validate the design before implementation.

Undefined

If the design of the work is undefined, you probably know that you want to implement something new, but no one has determined what steps will get you there (or perhaps what the new work instructions will look like for the employees). For example, you may need to implement a new organizational structure due to changing customer needs, but this new structure has not been defined, nor has the actual work to be done by individuals within the new structure been defined.

When the design of the work is undefined, it is frequently the responsibility of the change team to work with employees, stakeholders, customers, and leadership to define the work required to deliver the change. Your team will need to spend the necessary time in this step to plan the work.

There are many tools available to help you define the work to be done. The design can come from observing the processes where the existing work takes place, eliciting ideas for improvements from employees who do the existing work, as well as understanding customer and stakeholder needs that exist. A pioneer in organizational development, Richard Beckhard, noted that "people support what they help create." Giving people the opportunity to design the work they will do within the Change Initiative will go a long way in gaining support from the employees involved in the change.

The following list highlights various tools you can use to help design the work. We present a thorough list here, but please don't be overwhelmed! Your team may not need to use any of these tools, or may only use one or two of them. Use whatever you need to design the work in a way that employees can easily understand how to do the work. Simple is good!

Process Map: A process map presents a visual representation of the steps of an identified process by primarily using arrows (to show flow), rectangles (to show process steps), and diamonds (to show decisions). A process map is helpful to understand the existing process. Once the *new* work steps have been defined or planned, they can be depicted by a process map to show employees how the new work will be done.

Work Instructions: Work instructions are known by many other names, such as standard work, standardized work, and standard operating proceudres. Whatever a given company may call them (and whatever their form), these are the documented procedures by which *those who do the work know how to perform it today and from which they can improve the work tomorrow.* The documented procedures are often paired with competency training. Your team may start with any existing instructions to better understand the way the work is currently being done. Once you have designed the new work your team will write instructions necessary for the employees to perform the tasks in the new process. (Additional information and training on documented work instructions can be found at the Lean Enterprise Institute website at lean.org.)

Value Stream Map: A value stream map (VSM) is a diagram that shows the steps involved in the process of providing value to the customer.

This differs from a process map because it often adds elements such as time between each process step, inventory levels, and information flow. A current state VSM shows how the process is functioning prior to the new change implementation. A future state VSM shows the new process. (For additional information on value stream mapping, you can reference the book *Learning to See* by John Shook and Mike Rother.)

Process Measurement/Key Metrics: It is helpful to understand the existing process performance metrics before developing your new process. These metrics will help you and your team set goals after the adoption of the new process as well as determine if the new process is delivering the intended value.

FMEA: The Failure Modes and Effects Analysis (FMEA) helps identify the possible failure modes in a process—or the ways that the existing (and new) process can potentially fail. The "effects" portion of the FMEA looks at the potential outcomes of the failures. The tool also prioritizes potential failures according to the seriousness of the consequences. You can use the FMEA to examine existing processes to identify the most critical potential failures in the existing process, and then apply it to the new process to determine whether any new potential failures will be introduced with the new procedures.

Surveys, Interviews, Focus Groups, and Observations: These are commonly used methods to collect data from leadership, employees, customers, or stakeholders. Use these to gain insights into the existing process as well as your team members' expectations of the future process.

Each of the tools serves specific (and different) purposes. Be sure to choose the tool that is right for your situation.

Whether the Change Initiative is something that you will develop from its infancy, or you have been handed it in a ready-to-implement stage, the Change Questions will help you and your team consider the many aspects of the change. This includes things such as:

1. Who will be involved/affected by the change and what are their perceptions about the change?
2. What current practices and processes exist relating to the change?
3. How do the employees who do the existing work now believe the new work should be designed?
4. What are the customers' needs?
5. What tools can you use to design the new work?

You can think of these considerations as the context in which the change is taking place. Several researchers have found that an understanding of context is critical to successful change.

Accordingly, context has long been included as an important consideration in change implementation models. The Nadler-Tushman model urges organizations to understand: the work itself, the people who perform the work, the organizational structure, and the culture and operating environment. Nadler-Tushman viewed these elements as an interactive system which have enormous impact on the success or failure of the change.

Every change has its own challenges and complexities. Your team should gather enough information to have a working knowledge of the context to design the change's work. You will have the opportunity to gather additional situational data in a later stage of the Change Questions through methods such as conducting experiments, holding pilots, or launching simulations.

DESIGN THE WORK—HOW TO DO IT

Designing the Work of the Change Initiative

*I*n my early interviews with UP, I was initially told that the Lean design of the work was undefined. The Mechanical Department, which was responsible for locomotive repair and maintenance, had experimented with Lean, but it was my understanding that I had the support to build the Lean approach that I felt would be the most successful at UP. This was exciting for me because I had spent most of my career in continuous improvement (CI) but had primarily inherited existing programs that I could only tweak. The opportunity to start from scratch was a key reason that I accepted this position.

Shortly after I started at UP, I scheduled a meeting with the head of the Mechanical Department to better understand the department's approach to Lean. As I left for the meeting, one of the people in the CI department warned me that there was an ongoing feud between the mechanical and CI departments. The disagreement stemmed from the fact that mechanical was the only area in the Operating Department that had implemented Lean principles. Misha, the leader of the mechanical unit felt that the CI team should all be using Lean methodologies rather than the existing practice of letting each CI employee do his or her own thing. Even though I had one hour scheduled for my meeting with Misha, I was told, "Misha will probably kick you out after a few minutes because he doesn't like CI." In actuality, Misha and I hit it off. We were very aligned on the way we approached Lean, and I was thrilled to see that there was a Lean success story already in existence at UP.

To better understand the Lean approach in the Mechanical Department, the change team set up several sessions with mechanical employees who were doing their version of Lean (called UP Way). We visited them in the locomotive *repair shops and saw UP Way at work. We saw that the mechanical team members were truly passionate about UP Way. They were running their department with UP Way principles and were seeing tremendous success in terms of employee engagement and operational results.*

The department was using five elements of Lean. If you are not familiar with Lean, you may want to refer to definitions of these elements as you follow UP's story. (Various definitions of these Lean elements abound in organizations, and some vary slightly from the ones we used at UP.).

UP Way Elements

Standard Work and Leader Standard Work

- *Standard work: Operations are performed in a consistent manner and are regularly improved by the employees doing the work.*
- *Leader standard work: Leaders approach their roles with the form of standard work that includes mentoring and accountability.*

5S Workplace Organization

- *The workplace is cleaned and organized in a systematic manner.*

Visual Management

- *Visual work cues are in the workplace to provide process and performance information for all employees.*

Value Stream Mapping

- *Map-like illustrations are used that show the flow of process, materials, cycle times, and additional information such as inventory levels.*

Problem Solving

- *A standard process is used to analyze problems, determine root causes, and identify solutions.*

I was surprised to see such a well-defined Lean approach at UP. To be honest, I was also somewhat disappointed because again, I was looking forward to an opportunity to start from scratch. I didn't fault the CEO and COO as misrepresenting the situation. Instead, I realized that although they were aware of Misha's activities at a high level, they did not have granular information about the existing Lean activities in the department.

Along with exploring Lean within the department, I sought to understand the CI department's approach. As Misha had mentioned, the department had not adopted a common Lean methodology. The team members were physically scattered across the twenty-three states where UP operated and worked in their own geographic territories using whatever methodology worked for them to improve operating processes. They were passionate about improvement but didn't want to converge on one methodology for improvement. As I got to know the members of the team, I realized that they were hard-working, enthusiastic people who truly wanted the best thing for UP. The challenge was to get alignment on what was best for UP.

There were a few additional challenges:

- *The liaison who was assigned to help me understand the Operating Department at UP, as well as to help with implementation of Lean, had spent his entire career at UP and did not have much exposure to Lean. He had taken a university class on Lean but when I discussed specific proposals with him on how I envisioned Lean at UP, he told me that some of the things that I wanted to do were not in line with Lean principles presented in the class he had taken.*

- *Misha had developed a Lean guidebook, called The UP Way Handbook, which was different from the handbook that the former leader of the CI department had developed, which was different from the handbook my liaison in the Operating Department had started writing. Who knew that so many people wanted to write a handbook on Lean? Each was certain that his handbook was the one that UP should adopt. In fact, they were all different from what I would write if I were to create the handbook!*

- *The CI department that reported to me consisted of the people I would need to help drive the adoption of UP Way across the company. I knew that to be successful, everyone in CI had to accept Lean as the CI methodology. The preliminary relationship with my three direct reports was complicated by the fact that some of them had interviewed for the position I now had. I initially experienced a bit of resentment from some of them, which I attributed to this situation. One person, in particular, was vehemently opposed to one of the early changes I wanted to make, which was to establish metrics for success and track progress toward those metrics. I incorrectly assumed his resistance to my changes came from his disappointment at not getting the job. In fact, his resistance was from a "pure place" of a philosophical difference of opinion. Once I realized this, I respected his opinion and the passion with which he stuck to it, and we found a common ground to move forward. He became one of the biggest supporters of the change.*

Yes, this was a messy situation. However, it is rare (or non-existent) for a Change Initiative to have the unanimous support of all parties involved (remember Machiavelli?). Even if you are told (as I was) that the change is straightforward and completely supported, you have the responsibility to understand the context thoroughly before beginning implementation, and to expect resistance and nonalignment.

I was faced with some major decisions to make. The biggest decision was whether I was going to plow ahead with my own beliefs of what UP Way should look like, or whether I was going to integrate my ideas with the ideas of some of the key stakeholders within the initiative. On a personal level, I felt as if I had been brought in for the specific purpose of implementing Lean at UP because I had been doing it for most of my career. I wondered if I would be compromising the initiative if I implemented something other than what my experience led me to believe was the best way to approach Lean at UP.

These were some of my apprehensions:

■ *I had real concerns about the order in which the Mechanical Department implemented the five UP Way elements that it had chosen as the mainstay of its Lean approach. I had been successful in the past starting with two or three basic Lean tools to build quick successes and employee engagement. One of the five UP Way tools within mechanical was problem solving, which can become quite complex when trying to find the root cause of a problem. I felt that it may be overwhelming to introduce all five tools at the same time.*

■ *To be honest, I just didn't like the name "UP Way." I felt that it was copying The Toyota Way, and I would have preferred to create our own name that could also be uplifting and motivational. "Up" Way might have worked for me in terms of being uplifting, but since the common way to abbreviate UP was to use the letters U-P, I felt that the name didn't have the panache I would have wanted.*

Bottom line? I had to deal with my ego in that I felt that the people at UP weren't giving me credit for my expertise. I came in pretty much expecting them to adopt everything I suggested and was stunned that they weren't wowed enough by my credentials to do so—welcome to the real world!

I began engaging members of the CI group and the change team to help design the UP Way approach, with a strong focus on keeping key elements intact which were already working well in the Mechanical Department. As CI saw the successes in the department, it began to be more open to using many of the tools that the department was using. After much work, compromising, and partnering, we ended up with a consolidated version of UP Way to use. It had some existing elements of mechanical's Lean approach, such as the UP Way name and the five elements that the department considered fundamental. These were combined with some elements that were important to CI, such as certain training materials and mentoring functions. We also integrated one of the things that was important to me, which was tracking results! You can probably see that if I had ignored context when designing the work, this initiative would likely have failed. Later in this chapter, we discuss how to expect conflict and ways to resolve it, and more information on how the UP situation was resolved.

DO THE WORK, PART 1—WHAT TO DO

Change Question

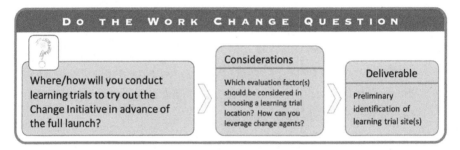

Figure 3.5: Do the Work Change Question

Learning Trials

Notice in this phase of PDCA, you want to "try the idea." Rather than implement an untested change across an entire organization, we recommend running some kind of learning trial in the form of a pilot, experiment, or simulation. There is only one way to fully know how your organization will react to a change: try it and see! This of course leads us to the common question: where exactly do we start?

Let's explore the UP experience (with further information on learning trials that follow the UP example).

Learning trial definition: a designated pilot, simulation, or experiment used to try out a new way of doing things.

DO THE WORK, PART 1—HOW TO DO IT

Doing the Work

To introduce the importance of a learning trial, I'll share one of my early failures, which for me reinforced the need to try out the change, before full implementation. Before I came to UP, I was working at Textron and was responsible for identifying and implementing Change Initiatives across seven business units operating in thirty-two different countries. I admit I had become a bit arrogant as the success and sustainment of the Change Initiatives steadily increased over the years. Even though I had developed my version of the Change Questions, I decided not to use a learning trial during one particular change that I was in the process of implementing. This change seemed easy to implement as it only affected a small number of people—albeit across all seven business units and in at least ten countries—and I had been successful in leading change with this group in the past. I felt that I had their trust and didn't have to go through the steps before implementation. At my peril, I didn't remember Machiavelli's words, "It must be remembered that there is nothing more difficult to plan, more doubtful of success, nor more dangerous to manage than a new order of things."

I rolled out the "new order of things" to all of the individuals involved in the change, and within a few days my email and voicemail were clogged with reasons why the change would not work and why some business units were not going to implement it. The pushback was extraordinarily strong and seemingly out of proportion to a change that I perceived as minor. How did I respond? I decided to research reasons why this change failed.

During my research, I discovered the 20-60-20 rule. The rule asserted that 20 percent of the people will be negative about whatever aspect is being considered, 60 percent will be neutral, and 20 percent will be positive. The researchers set out to determine whether the popular belief that splits the population into three groups had mathematical credibility. The rule had been widely publicized before this study as applicable to things as diverse as performance management in organizations, reception of speakers within various audiences, and acceptance of people to change.

The researchers proposed that this ratio implied some sort of natural balance, and so they decided to test the theory. They found that the 20-60-20 rule was supported mathematically in most circumstances. Further studies have replicated this original one, and the rule has been widely referenced in subsequent years in discussing change management and in other related fields.

Anecdotally, I have also found that when applied to change, in any given group, approximately 20 percent of people are positive about the change. These people are often known as "change agents." Approximately the same percentage of people are negative about the change—this can range from passive resistance to active resistance. The middle 60 percent are neutral. The neutral group may go through the motions of change, but usually wait before they fully commit to the change—and this is important—until they can determine if it will be worth the effort.

20-60-20 Curve

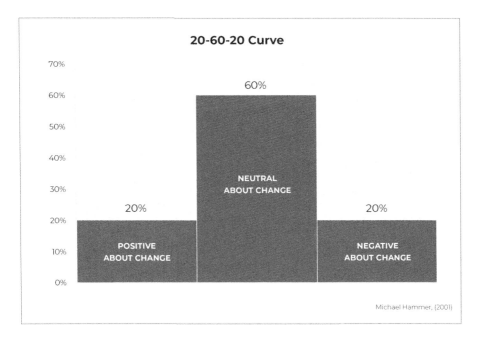

Figure 3.6: 20-60-20 Curve

While I was mulling this over, after being slammed with resistance from the change I had initiated, I spent a weekend at a friend's house on Martha's Vineyard. During a walk, we looked down the side of a cliff toward a beach and I noticed a very odd thing. There was a group of people in their swimsuits walking along the beach, which was shaped like a half-moon bay. They started at one end of the bay and walked all the way to the other end. Given that the beach was completely empty, I was puzzled as to why they had seemingly rejected most of the pristine beach, only to stop at one of the furthest points from where they started. I mentioned this to my friend, and she immediately said that they were headed for the rip tide. I always thought that a rip tide would carry people out to sea, but my friend said that this rip tide was gentle and would carry people to the other side of the bay.

As we talked, I noticed that the first swimmer made a big production of getting a running start and diving right in. Once he got in, he swam aggressively and moved swiftly and smoothly through the water. Another person followed him. Next came the majority of people who plopped into their inner tubes and floated along with little to no effort. Finally, there were only a few people left. One of them took several tentative steps and then turned quickly around and made his way back to shore. This small group walked around the bay to meet their friends on the other side. Suddenly I realized that the 20-60-20 curve had played itself out right before my eyes. I immediately understood my mistake in the implementation of the change I had just initiated! I forgot that more likely than not, only 20 percent of the people would be open to the change.

*The takeaway here is that without any mitigation to this effect, the natural instincts of these three groups may well prevail. There will be people who actively resist even the simplest change, and conversely, there will be people who willingly accept even the most difficult change. I have seen this occur again and again. **I began to understand the need to target change through a learning trial such as a pilot, simulation, or experiment, especially focused on people who are open to change.***

DO THE WORK, PART 2—WHAT TO DO

The Need for a Learning Trial

Think about how change is usually implemented. Generally, it is rolled out across organizations. A typical implementation plan may look like this:

- June 1: announce the change to all employees.
- June 30: implement the change with all employees.

When an organization attempts to roll out a change across the board without a learning trial such as a pilot, simulation, or experiment, the initiative almost always has major missteps. It could be that people are not trained correctly, the necessary forms are missing, or the IT system doesn't work the way it is expected to. There are plenty of opportunities to miss potential problems in a large-scale change implementation—or even a small-scale change. Without a learning trial, problems are not discovered until implementation. Once significant problems occur, the people who resist change have additional ammunition to shoot down the change and negatively influence the people who are neutral.

Both the need to build positive momentum and to work out the missteps have led us to run learning trials before widespread introduction. In fact, we often run more than one experimental activity. We strongly encourage you and your team to explore various ways to experiment or "test the solution(s)" before full-scale introduction of the initiative.

In this chapter, we will expand in greater detail on selecting a learning trial in the form of a pilot, as it has multiple advantages as a way to test the solution. Of course, sometimes it is not possible to run a pilot. In these instances, we encourage your team to think of creative ways to run a simulation, where you continue to do things the old way but have some people simulate the new processes. You can also break the solution into a series of smaller experiments which are then simulated or piloted. In Lean Manufacturing terminology, these learning trials are often known as a "model line," "model area," or "learning line."

The following UP story describes an extensive process used to choose the learning trial. We had twenty-two sites to choose from and had to objectively evaluate each site to determine which ones would give us the greatest probability of success. When you use the Change Questions framework for yourself, you can skip the evaluation step if you don't have multiple options as to where you can run your learning trial.

Major initiatives typically entail discovery that is broader than procedural missteps such as missing forms or difficult IT systems. It is important to remember that the discovery that emerges in learning trials can change the intended solution. This is not necessarily a bad thing. We have been in situations where we have discovered a better solution than the original solution by, for example, simply gathering employee feedback while running a learning trial. Just as you ask your team members to keep an open mind, it is critical that you do so as well and that you model this for your change team.

In future chapters, we will expand on activities to help you and your change team maximize the value of the learning trial, including ways to create buy-in when you're implementing the Change Initiative in areas that are led by people who are uncomfortable with change.

Purpose of learning trials: identify improvement opportunities for the Change Initiative before full implementation.

DO THE WORK, PART 2—HOW TO DO IT

Identifying Learning Trial Locations

*A*fter designing the new work to be done and examining the options available as to where we could do the new work, our change team determined that the best way to test solutions and gather feedback would be to identify several learning trial sites.

We realized that unlike some organizations, we had multiple sites available to us—twenty-two, in fact. UP's Operating Department was segmented into three geographic regions (north, south, and west). The regions were divided into twenty-two service units and each one represented a broad spectrum of the functions of the Operating Department. Therefore, we identified each service unit as a potential learning trial location. We decided that we would choose one service unit within each region which would provide us with three learning trial locations.

Figure 3.7: UP's Potential Learning Trial Locations

Our change team then brainstormed factors to help us choose the optimal learning trial site(s). We determined that location was one factor to consider. We would prefer a site located within one hour of an airport since many people would be traveling to and from the site to participate in the learning trial. Another factor was the makeup of the employees in the learning trial. We needed a site with good representation across the majority of the functional areas in the Operating Department. We then evaluated each site based on our evaluation factor criteria and identified the sites that met our criteria, service units 2 and 3.

UP's Potential Learning Trial Locations (partial listing)				
Identify potential learning trial locations	Service Unit 1	Service Unit 2	Service Unit 3	Service Unit 4
Evaluation factor 1: **Location** (within 1 hour of airport)	2 hours	15 minutes	45 minutes	1.5 hours
Evaluation factor 2: **Representative Employees** (At least 4 employee groups represented at site)	4 Employee Groups	5 Employee Groups	5 Employee Groups	3 Employee Groups

Figure 3.8: UP's Evaluation of Potential Learning Trial Locations

Notice that the evaluation factors we used were quantifiable. This made it easy to evaluate but didn't give us the full picture. In the next section, we will incorporate the 20-60-20 change curve concepts to show you how UP finalized the learning trial sites.

DO THE WORK, PART 3—WHAT TO DO

Target Change Agents with Learning Trials

Your Change Initiative will have a higher probability of success if you can incorporate the lessons from the 20-60-20 model into the process of finalizing your learning trial location(s). If you ignore this change-agent factor and initiate your learning trial with people who naturally resist change, there is a higher probability that your learning trial will fail, thus making it harder for the change to be successful. We still recommend involving people who resist the change in your initiative because it can make your initiative stronger. But it's all about timing. Early on, you will want to seek out change agents within learning trials to build positive momentum to influence the neutral majority and increase your probability of sustaining the change.

Positive momentum is propelled through positive feedback and good results that flow from the early learning trial(s). Conversely, negative momentum will be generated by early failures, which will influence the middle 60 percent neutral majority, making it very difficult to turn the negative momentum around. Once you have created positive momentum in your Change Initiative, you can then turn the attention to the 20 percent of the people who may naturally resist the change—in a respectful and listening manner.

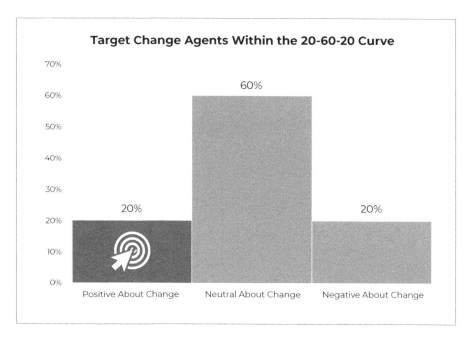

Figure 3.9: Target Change Agents Within the 20-60-20 Curve

We understand that making the change-agent designation a key factor for choosing the learning trial location may not be the most common approach, and it may not always be possible. Before we understood the research on the importance of change agents (expanded on in Chapter 4), we would choose learning trial sites solely based on other factors such as the cost to run the trial, the department with the biggest impact, or the most convenient location (to make traveling easier on people!). All these considerations are important, but they are secondary to the change-agent designation. In this section, we will harness the power of change agents to create a successful Change Initiative.

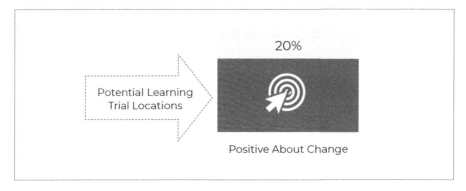

Figure 3.10: Potential Learning Trial Locations

**Change agent definition: A person who acts as a catalyst
for a new way of doing things.**

If you ask a group of people to identify change agents within an organization, they will usually have no trouble in coming up with specific names. In reviewing studies that identify characteristics of successful change agents, the following traits typically show up:

- Open-minded,
- Listens,
- Takes responsibility,
- Motivates people,
- Flexible,
- Results focused,
- Respected/trusted.

You will notice that some of these characteristics encompass the individual's openness to change and others cover the individual's ability to make change happen. Sometimes, we interpret someone's ability to be an effective change agent simply based on that person's *openness/willingness* to change. Individuals may be open to change, but not skilled in planning the change, delivering results, or motivating others. We encourage you to think about all aspects of successful change agents when considering where you decide to start your learning trials.

DO THE WORK, PART 3—HOW TO DO IT

Change Agents and Learning Trials

*W*e were now ready to finalize the best loca-tions for the learning trials considering employee engagement and the 20-60-20 model. Our change team identified the leaders of each ser-vice unit as shown in the following chart (Daniel, Olivia, Prathna, and Zhang). Of that list, the change team determined that both Daniel and Prathna had the characteristics of successful change agents. When reviewing all the critical factors, the table shows that only Prathna had the right location, good representation across her employee group, and change-agent characteristics. Prathna led service unit three, so we chose that service unit for our learning trial in the western region. We repeated this process for the other two regions to obtain one learning trial for each of the three regions.

Finalizing UP Way Learning Trial Location (partial listing)				
Identify potential learning trial locations	Service Unit 1	Service Unit 2	Service Unit 3	Service Unit 4
Evaluation factor 1: **Location** (within 1 hour of airport)	**2 hours**	15 minutes	45 minutes	**1.5 hours**
Evaluation factor 2: **Representative Employees** (At least 4 employee groups represented at site)	4 Employee Groups	5 Employee Groups	5 Employee Groups	**3 Employee Groups**
Identify the leader (by name) of each functional area. Circle or color code Change Agents.	Daniel Fuller	**Olivia Linn**	Prathna Moore	**Zhang Wei**

Figure 3.11: Finalizing UP Way Learning Trial Location

IMPROVE THE WORK—WHAT TO DO

Change Question

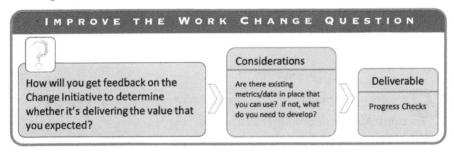

Figure 3.12: Improve the Work Change Question

Learn and Improve

You can't improve the work without checking how the process is performing. As employees are doing the work, a measurement should be occurring, which is the check. Before having employees do the work, it is critical to determine what you are going to measure and how you are going to measure it. We call this measurement a progress check. Most organizations ignore this step of the process, and by doing so, often have poorer results from the initiative than those organizations that form a feedback loop of designing, doing, measuring, improving, and repeating.

In a study of 343 companies, it was determined that most organizations deploy Change Initiatives in a method that the researchers coined "operational speed." The authors defined operational speed as establishing a timeline for the initiative, then moving quickly according to that set timeline. Success was measured by meeting the timeline milestones. Alternatively, a few of the 343 companies deployed their Change Initiatives by utilizing "strategic speed." This was identified as moving at the speed necessary to deliver value with regular feedback loops to adjust the initiatives as needed. Over three years, the companies that used strategic speed averaged 52 percent better results than those companies that utilized the operational speed model.

What do we mean by *deliver value* here? Recall that within the purpose section of the Change Questions, you created value statements to identify the benefit you expect to gain from the initiative. At this point in the change process, you will want to pair those value statements with feedback loops—or progress checks to measure if the change is delivering the value you anticipated.

Value Statement: A sentence that <u>describes the expected benefit</u> that the Change Initiative should deliver.

Progress Check: A <u>measurement</u> activity, either existing or new, that provides feedback on the <u>amount of expected value</u> to be derived from the Change Initiative.

Note that the value statement differs from the progress check in that it describes the expected benefit in a sentence format, whereas the progress check actually measures the quantitative amount of the expected benefit. Recall that the value statements described in the previous chapter were specific and measurable. When creating the measurable portion of the value statement, we loosely defined measurable. In the examples given in the previous chapter, "customer interactions" and "yard dwell time" were identified as examples of what was being measured. However, the actual metric that would be used was undefined. That's where the progress check comes in.

Sometimes it is difficult to measure the amount of expected value, so it is mistakenly substituted for a progress check that is "value lite" or doesn't represent the value at all. For example, let's say that you are going to implement a new billing system. You may decide to train hundreds of people throughout the world to use the new billing system. One of the easiest progress checks to get is:

- The number of people trained to use the new billing system

However, is that the *value* you expect to get from the system—people who are trained in the new system? What if they are poorly trained,

trained but don't use the new system, use it incorrectly, or the system doesn't deliver the value you expected it to deliver? You won't detect any of that if your only progress check is simply the number of people trained. It is reasonable to keep track of the number of people trained, but let's not kid ourselves into thinking that once all the people are trained in the new system, the Change Initiative will automatically deliver value. Let's up the game to:

- The number of people using the new billing system

OK—we're getting closer! Now you know how many people are actually using the new system. However, you can tell that we haven't gotten there yet—for example, what if they're using it incorrectly or the new system is generating more errors than the old system?

Remember, the first step in the strategic speed concept is to determine the value you expect to get from the change. Ultimately, in this example, if you expect that the new billing system will reduce billing errors, the progress check should measure the number of billing errors using the old system versus the number of errors using the new system with the goal of reducing the errors.

Value Statement	Progress Check
The new billing system will reduce the number of billing errors.	Number of billing errors (pre-training minus post-training)

Figure 3.13: Billing Example Value Statement and Progress Check

Unless you can get that information electronically, it may not be an easy progress check to implement. Despite the difficulty, it's essential to develop a progress check that measures the value itself—otherwise, you may be wasting the energy of a lot of people. If it is impossible to get this information electronically, there are other methods you can use. For example, you can ask employees to keep a log for a brief period or observe employees in a non-judgmental manner to understand billing accuracy. If you choose change agents to lead the learning trials, employees will most likely be open to observation, especially if you ask them to share their ideas and suggestions to help improve the process before it's introduced to the entire organization.

Some commonly used progress checks to gain feedback on a value statement are surveys, observations, focus groups, interviews, operational metrics, time metrics, or savings metrics. Your change team will define the progress check in this step and develop the actual progress check tools if the measurements don't already exist.

Value Statement	Progress Check
The new organizational chart will streamline customer interactions	■ Customer satisfaction survey results ■ Number of customer "touch points" ■ Time involved to resolve customer issues
Value Statement	**Progress Check**
The new process for switching railcars will reduce yard dwell time	■ Dwell time metrics (pre-post)

Figure 3.14: Examples of Value Statements and Progress Checks

When to Perform a Progress Check

If an organization's change activity is going to ultimately fail, research has shown that failure can be detected as early as one month after the kick-off. At that point in time, a trend among both top-performing and less successful groups reveals itself. The trend in the less successful group is that employee commitment and support for the change begins to subside, while the more successful change organizations show increased employee commitment during the first month. Think about that! Wouldn't you want to know right away if your initiative was struggling?

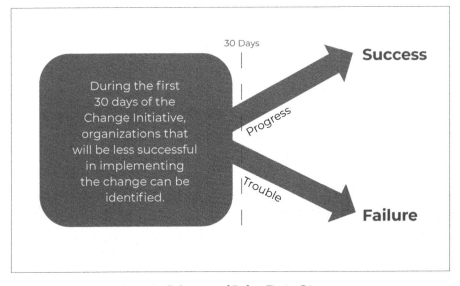

Figure 3.15: Success and Failure Timing Diagram

It is critical to develop the progress check tools before the learning trial begins. These tools should be ready to launch within the first month of your learning trial. Your change team will use the progress checks to obtain feedback until you can be assured that the change has taken hold.

Using Feedback to Adjust

When you obtain information from the progress check you will be able to learn from this information and make improvements as necessary. This is the "act" in the PDCA cycle. You will also be able to evaluate if you're on track or if the initiative is heading toward failure. If you find that there are indications of potential failure, you can then determine if there are existing obstacles that are preventing it from succeeding. It could be that the IT system doesn't allow employees to use the new process, or the instructions for implementing the change aren't clear. Perhaps you need to modify or add training. You can use these new learnings to improve the overall design of the change.

You can often detect problems in advance that could prohibit the change from being effective; however, it is likely that even with this step in the Change Questions, you may miss a few obstacles, which you can then detect in the learning trials through—you guessed it—a progress check!

Another potential failure that the progress check may reveal involves individuals who are opposed to the change. Leaders who are opposed to the adoption of the change may give "lip service" to imitate their support of the change, but when they are with their employees, they deliver an entirely different message. This is difficult to detect without a method to do so. You will see a few examples of ways to uncover a lack of leadership support in the UP story. If you find that leaders are resisting the change, you may need to take the time to understand the resistance and see if the initiative needs to be adjusted or if your leaders need additional support, coaching, or other resources/actions.

The progress check also has a positive purpose. It detects strengths and successes. These can be used to set up benchmark partnerships where you pair a potential failure with a success and allow the struggling organization to correct its course. The progress check also helps you identify success stories that can be incorporated into your communication plan or highlighted in the recognition activities we talk about in the next chapter.

As a reminder, at this point in the Change Questions process, you are still planning the Change Initiative. This section is intended for your change team to begin to identify the learning trial location. The actual implementation will occur later.

IMPROVE THE WORK—HOW TO DO IT

Improving the Work

UP defined the five value statements for the UP Way as:

1. Empowered employees are improving customer service.
2. UP Way activities in the field improve safety and operational performance.
3. Employees are skilled in UP Way concepts and are using them in the workplace.
4. Training people in UP Way problem solving tools is building a problem solving culture.
5. Employee involvement in UP Way increases employee engagement.

By breaking each of the five value statements into progress checks, we realized that we had to measure:

1. Customer service,
2. Safety and operational performance,
3. Employees' skills and use of UP Way concepts,
4. The culture of UP as it relates to problem solving by employees,
5. Employee engagement.

We used these value statements to help us develop our progress checks. Initially, we didn't expect some of these metrics to show up right away—especially during the learning trials, as things like customer satisfaction and safety are often slow-moving metrics. This didn't stop us from including them.

The UP story presents several examples of ways to use progress checks. Feel free to copy the UP methods or create your own. Also, remember that the UP Way initiative was complex and far-reaching. Therefore, the progress checks had to be fairly extensive. If your change is occurring in one small department *or on one piece of equipment in a factory, you will have a much-simplified progress check approach.*

The change team matched each value statement with pre-planned ways to measure the value with a progress check. Whenever possible, we tried to use existing metrics. For example, the measurements that UP already had in place were:

- *Customer service metrics,*
- *Operational results,*
- *Safety performance results,*
- *Annual engagement survey scores.*

The progress checks that the change team had to develop were:

- *Pre-post training surveys,*
- *Panel survey,*
- *Number of active UP Way projects led by employees,*
- *Sustainment metrics of UP Way projects.*

Value Statement	Progress Check
Empowered employees are engaged in improving customer service.	■ Panel Survey ■ Customer Service Metrics
UP Way improves safety and operational performance.	■ Pre-Post Training Surveys ■ Panel Survey ■ Operational Results ■ Safety Performance Results
Employees are skilled in UP Way concepts and are using them in the workplace.	■ Pre-Post Training Surveys ■ Panel Survey
We are building a problem-solving culture.	■ Number of active UP Way projects led by employees ■ Results metrics of UP Way projects ■ Sustainment metrics of UP Way projects
UP Way builds employee engagement.	■ Pre-Post Training Surveys ■ Annual Engagement Survey Scores ■ Panel Survey

Figure 3.16: UP's Value Statements and Progress Checks

The first progress check we created measured the effectiveness of the UP Way employee training. One of the ways we found to demonstrate leadership commitment to the initiative was to expect that each leader would train his or her employees in the UP Way. However, since most leaders were not instructors by trade, it was critical to ensure that the concepts were taught effectively. We created a progress check around training and provided a CI specialist to assist the leaders during the training.

The students in each class completed the following four-question survey at the end of each training session. We gathered the data anonymously, but we kept it categorized by class. The classes were then matched with the instructor, who was also their workplace manager.

Training Survey

On a scale of 1 to 6, with 1 being "strongly disagree" and 6 being "strongly agree," please respond to the following statements:
1. I understand the concept.
2. I have the skills to apply the concept.
3. I understand how the concept will improve the workplace.
4. I believe that the concept will increase employee engagement.

The topics we covered are as follows. We briefly described these concepts earlier in this chapter:
1. Standard work,
2. 5S workplace organization,
3. Visual management,
4. Value stream mapping,
5. Problem solving.

We used these classroom surveys to begin to gather data on four elements of the value statements in this phase of our progress check.

UP's Training Survey Supports Value Statements

Survey Immediately Following Training	Value Statement
I understand (concept).	Employees' skill
I have the skills to apply (concept).	Employees' use of UP Way
I understand how (concept) will improve the workplace.	Safety and Operational Performance
I believe that (concept) will increase employee engagement.	Employee Engagement

Figure 3.17: How UP's Training Survey Supports Value Statements

The first survey was given immediately after the training and the results were encouraging. We found that the overall average of the classes was a 5 out of 6, which equated to "agree" with the statements. In other words, most employees surveyed agreed that they understood UP Way concepts, believed they had the skills to use the concepts, understood how the concepts would improve their workplace, and felt that the concepts would improve employee engagement.

We also used these results to evaluate the ability of the managers to teach the UP Way. Some classes scored significantly lower than the overall average, and some scored significantly higher than the average. The results were used to coach the instructors/managers whose classes scored poorly. We identified managers who had high scores and asked them to serve as coaches for some of the lower-scoring managers. We were also able to use recognition tools (covered in the next chapter) to publicize the early successes of the high-scoring managers.

The second part of the survey was conducted two to four months later. Students received a slightly revised survey to complete. For example, instead of the statement "I believe I have the skills to utilize the (concept) in my workplace," we asked them to respond to the statement "I have applied the (concept) in my workplace."

UP's Training Survey Comparisons

Survey Immediately Following Training	Survey 2-4 Months Following Training
I understand (concept).	I understand (concept).
I have the skills to apply (concept).	I <u>have applied</u> (concept).
I understand how (concept) will improve the workplace.	(Concept) <u>has improved</u> my workplace.
I believe that (concept) will increase employee engagement.	(Concept) <u>has increased</u> employee engagement.

Figure 3.18: UP's Training Survey Comparisons

Like the first survey, the second linked trainees with their managers and was anonymous on an individual respondent basis. In the initial survey, we measured the manager's teaching skills, but in this second survey several months later, we measured if the manager had created the environment and opportunity to use UP Way. Also note that in the first survey, Q4 only asked employees if they believed that the concept would increase employee engagement. The second survey, given two to four months following the training, asked if the employees felt that the UP Way had increased employee engagement. In some cases—especially with operating performance—it was too early to know if the

UP Way had actually improved some of these areas, but shortly you will read how we ultimately were able to match this information with tangible results.

The following chart shows the overall average of all managers/instructors and their employees' responses. When we received the second survey's responses, we matched the averages by manager with their first responses. The overall results of the classes were encouraging, as the second survey still scored an average of 5 meaning the employees retained agreement with all of the statements.

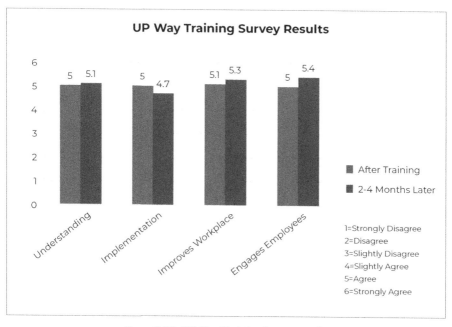

Figure 3.19: UP Way Training Survey Results

Overall Results

Immediately after Training:

- Employees "agreed" that they understood the concepts and could implement them, which would improve employee engagement and departmental results.

2 to 4 Months after Training:

■ Employees "agreed" that they had implemented UP Way, it had improved employee engagement, and it had improved operating results.

The richness of the data was revealed when we looked at each comparison group by individual manager/instructor. We could determine the sites that did not implement UP Way, or the sites that implemented it, but where employees didn't believe UP Way improved the workplace or increased employee engagement. Again, we followed up on these learnings with observational fact-finding, improvements to our approach in sharing these new ways of working and coaching for the manager.

In addition to insights we gained from the surveys, they provided a built-in reinforcement mechanism. Managers knew that we would be evaluating their ability to train employees, thus they had an incentive to train as well as they could. They were also aware that we would be asking their employees if UP Way had been implemented. This gave them additional motivation to ensure that the employees were given opportunities and encouragement to use UP Way concepts.

Approximately two to three months into UP Way activities, we had trained 5 percent of the 42,000 workforce and fixed many of the problems that arose. We had data that identified where UP Way was working, and where we needed to focus more effort. At this point, we continued the progress-checking activity throughout the remainder of the training. If this was all that we did, however, we still lacked sufficient feedback to ensure that UP Way was sustaining long-term, nor did we have robust answers to the value statements relating to the effect UP Way had on things like operating results, customer satisfaction, and employee engagement.

For our next progress check, we stole a concept from the medical field. Most people are familiar with longitudinal studies within healthcare where, for example, people who have a certain heart condition may be given a new drug and then studied for some time. This method of choosing a group of people who are studied for a fairly long timeframe is called a longitudinal study or panel survey. We decided to apply this concept by creating something that we called the UP Way panel survey.

We needed to understand the effectiveness of the change implementation on 42,000 employees. If we tried to survey each of those 42,000 employees, given the fact that railroad employees are never together under the same roof, and generally work in small teams or crews of two people, we would be lucky to get a 20 percent response rate.

Response rate is a big deal. People who respond are usually different from the people who don't respond. The responders usually have the strongest feelings and generally the most negative feelings. It is misleading to take the results of a survey with a low response rate and extrapolate the results to everyone in the organization. Yet, that's what many organizations do. We decided to take a different approach. We decided to randomly select the employees who would form the panel study and aggressively follow up with them to get a high response rate. If we could deliver on that, we could make inferences back to the entire organization with much more confidence.

We calculated the statistical sample size that would allow us to make inferences back to our 42,000 operating employees. The calculated sample size was approximately 350 people. We rounded up to 400 people. We randomly chose 400 people in the sample in such a way that they matched the demographics of our overall Operating Department. So, for example, if 10 percent of the department were conductors, then 10 percent of the employees in the sample were conductors. We contacted each of the 400 employees and asked them if they would commit to being a member of the panel survey for several years. We told them that they would be surveyed every six months for approximately three years. The survey would take them 10 minutes to complete, and their individual results would be kept confidential and only revealed in summary with other respondents.

Most people agreed to participate. We told them, "You're going to make a difference. You're going to be the person that represents people just like you *around the country, and we need to hear your voice." We meant it, and when I reflect on that time, I appreciate all the ways that our employees guided us into making UP Way better and better. The people that did not choose to participate in the survey were randomly replaced with somebody who had the same demographics as the person who declined participation. Much of the survey itself mirrored the value statements. It asked about employee engagement, customer satisfaction, operating results, use of UP Way concepts in the workplace, and leadership support. I think people had a sense we were listening to them and moving in a new and exciting direction that would not only make UP better but make their jobs better.*

UP Way Panel Survey Results

We were hoping to get at least an 85 percent response rate from our panel. We obtained response rates of over 90 percent for every one of the surveys sent to the panel participants over the four years that we utilized the panel survey. There were many significant results. We'll review just a few of them here. Since we had high response rates and had randomly chosen the participants in our panel study, we had the statistical ability to make inferences back to the entire Operating Department.

One year after launch, 39 percent of the employees in the Operating Department felt that they had benefited from at least one UP Way concept during the previous six months. By year three, 54 percent of the people said that they had benefited.

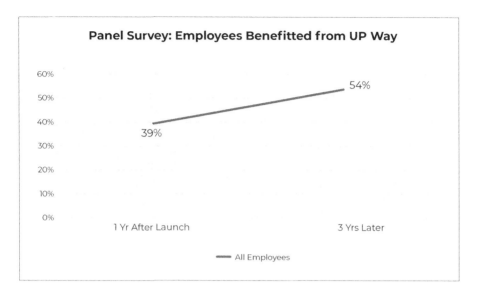

Figure 3.20: Panel Survey: Employees Benefitted from UP Way

By year four—and I think this is impressive—84 percent of all non-union employees in the Operating Department felt that they benefited from at least one UP Way concept during the previous six months, and 60 percent of the union employees felt the same.

In terms of specific UP Way concepts, at the end of year one, 31 percent of the union employees in the Operating Department said that they had used standard work during the previous six months, and 41 percent were using standard work three years later. This doesn't show as great of an increase as some of the other concepts. However, we were heartened that we continued to gain rather than lose ground. The results were more impressive for non-union employees. Sixty-seven percent of them were using standard work or leader standard work one year after launch, and 80 percent were using it three years after launch.

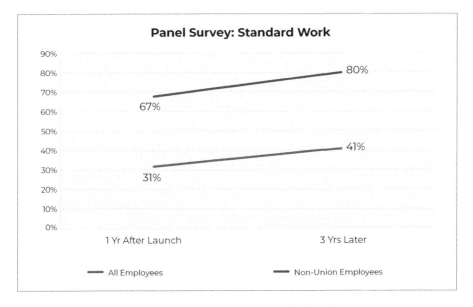

Figure 3.21: Panel Survey – Standard Work

UP Way Panel Survey Results Correlated with Operating Results

After the first year of the panel survey, we had enough data to begin to correlate UP Way scores with existing metrics including operating results. We created a composite score from the panel surveys that demonstrated the maturity of UP Way in each area in the Operating Department by using the pre-post training data and the panel survey data. We correlated that score with the business results from the operating KPI (key process indicator) scorecard of the various departments, sub-departments, and geographic areas in the department. We found no statistically significant correlation between UP Way maturity and operating results in years 1 and 2 and started to get worried.

Looking at the graphs and numbers in these first few years, however, we saw the numbers progressively heading in a positive direction. However, we held firm that we would wait for a statistically significant result because otherwise, there was a small probability that the improved scores were due to chance.

By year three, there was a statistically significant correlation between UP Way program's maturity and operating results. The highest-performing service units in terms of their operational metrics had the highest scores on UP Way maturity. Conversely, all the lowest-scoring service units in terms of operational results had the lowest UP Way scores. We found similar results when correlating other metrics such as employee engagement with UP Way maturity.

During the first two years when we were looking for statistically significant results, we also had some meaningful success stories which reinforced our confidence in UP Way. For example, UP had a certain service unit that consistently ranked at the bottom of the monthly operating results KPI report. Service unit leaders came and went to no avail. This particular service unit stubbornly remained at the bottom of the pack. The service unit leader invited us to send a team and help them engage with, understand, and ultimately implement UP Way. Within six months, the service unit went from the bottom of the operating results list to the top and remained in the top three service units for the next several years running.

Practical Application: Design, Do, and Improve the Work

The worst thing for trains, planes, and automobiles is when they sit and wait. On a train track, this is not just a problem for the first waiting train, but for all the trains queuing up behind the waiting train and becoming waiting trains themselves. This is especially a problem for the train engineers and conductors who are sitting on a waiting train, knowing they will miss a family meal or child's baseball game.

Rebecca decided to use UP Way to help address this problem. Originally, UP had utilized two metrics for measuring train delays: one that measured the excess time a train was stopped <u>in the terminal</u> for changing crews, refueling, etc. and the other for waiting time while it was stopped <u>between terminals.</u> The employees at the terminal were accountable for the first metric, called "dwell time," and the train dispatchers (think air traffic controllers for trains) were accountable for the latter which was called "road velocity." Sounds straightforward, right?

Oddly enough, when Rebecca began looking at the context around the metrics and observing the stopped trains in and around the terminals, she noticed something strange. She could see the dwell time as it occurred in real time within the metric, but it didn't match the actual situation in front of her. For example, she could see that there was often little to no wait time at the terminal according to the metric; however, her own eyes were seeing trains stacked up all over the place. The dispatchers blamed the delays on congestion in the terminal and the terminals pointed the finger at dispatchers for overloading the terminal area with "waves" of trains.

The finger-pointing and long-running disagreement between dispatch and the terminal existed because both groups knew what they were seeing—and they were seeing completely different things. Unfortunately, they were each being measured by different electronic dwell/velocity metrics and neither captured the whole picture.

Rebecca decided the first thing she had to do before she could even attempt to improve the process was to fix the measurement system. She formed a cross-functional team to create an accurate metric that included both the terminal and road wait times. Imagine if Rebecca had not observed this problem herself and had dug right into redesigning the work based on the flawed measurement system; it most likely would have been a waste of time.

Once the team fixed the measurement system, in part by establishing agreed-upon electronic fences in appropriate places around the terminal, they could start to apply UP Way techniques to redesign the work. It would have been so great—and so easy if the team could have designed the new work for one terminal and then dropped it into all the other terminals. No such luck! Each terminal had its specific circumstances, geography, infrastructure, and activities that made it necessary to design a unique solution. The team found that problems are often best addressed situationally as specific solutions applied in one place may not apply elsewhere.

The team worked with the terminal and dispatch employees who did the work and came up with solutions together. They then tried the solutions to see which ones would work best and found that learning trials were critical for the success of the new work. The team also found that embedding learning (and a process for learning) helped to sustain improvement. This was important, not only to make sure they had the best solutions but to overcome resistance. A couple of the refrains they heard were: "You don't understand, that's not how we do it on the railroad. Every day is different; we can't possibly design a standard way to do the work."

Of course, when there is no attempt to standardize the work, every day is different! As the learning trials gained traction, employees increasingly felt ownership of their work and their results. The team took the results of the learning trials and established standard work for the solutions that were most widely applicable. Improvement happened very quickly once the standard work was in place. This made things easier for employees within the terminal, and as the dwell time decreased, life got better for the engineers and conductors on the trains, confirming that stability is the foundation for improvement (as well as a better work life).

When Rebecca returned to one of the terminals to start looking at how she might continue to improve upon the new work, she was greeted by a group of union employees who couldn't wait to show her what they had done. They unveiled a video about dwell time which they had distributed to all the employees at the terminal. It not only covered how the new measurement system worked, but employees acted out the scenario of a person who had enthusiastically planned a big football party. He invited his friends, ordered a new large-scale TV to be delivered the day before the game, purchased the food and beer, and was just waiting for his TV to arrive. On the day of his big party, the TV was still a no-show. And where was it? The camera then zoomed to a train loaded with shipping containers stuck on the terminal's track, waiting … waiting … waiting … to move.

This team found a way to make dwell time personal for everyone in their terminal. We came to believe that personal ownership may be the most important ingredient for sustainable engagement and improvement everywhere! And the improvements didn't stop there. Once straightforward improvements were made and standardized, the terminals began to do in-depth problem solving to address more and more aspects of dwell time.

Dwell time continued to improve through several iterations of effort. Since the railroad is a complex system and interactions are plentiful among the various components of the system, the dwell time benefit at each terminal often multiplies down the line and shows up in metrics such as better customer service/on-time delivery, reduction in train line-up downline, and reductions in recrew rates.

2013: Completed eight dwell time projects that averaged a 19 percent improvement,

2014: Completed six dwell time projects that averaged a 9 percent improvement,

2015: Completed fifteen dwell time projects that averaged a 31 percent improvement,

2016: Completed twenty-six dwell time projects that averaged a 22 percent improvement,

2017: Completed eighteen dwell time projects that averaged an 18 percent improvement

Sometimes people think this kind of activity takes too much work. However, if the Change Initiative is important enough to expend energy on it, the extra effort it takes to ensure that it's working and is delivering true value is well worth it. You may also think that UP's progress checks—especially the four-year panel survey—are overkill. We agree that if your change is not complex or covers a small number of people, a panel survey is most likely more than you need. It's up to you and your change team to design the most appropriate progress checks for your situation. It's kind of like the Papa Bear, Mama Bear, and Baby Bear tale where Goldilocks struggled to find the just-right aspect of various things like food temperature, bed softness, and chair size. Your team should strive for not too much, not too little, but just right!

Lynn is describing her experience as the leader of a broad, formal Change Initiative at a large, very traditional, publicly owned corporation in what some would describe as an entrenched industry. Change doesn't always occur in such a setting, of course. You may be a first-line supervisor in a physical production facility or a software engineer designing the user interface for a new app or founder of a startup. The specific actions to be taken may vary (after all, the problem to solve is different), but the *thinking* as well as the general sets of considerations remain the same.

Ordinarily, for most of us, the place to assign our first attention is to the actual value-creating work of the enterprise. Turning the screw to fasten part to part; manipulating the scalpel to make the incision; sterilizing and returning surgical implements to the proper place for next usage; cooking the soup; writing the code (or literally typing in the code on the keyboard if that is what coders indeed do). It is the change of *that* work—its design, doing, and improving—that defines both the character and the value of any economic enterprise. I've found that the better we understand that work and the more methodical we are in improving it, the better the chances that we will ensure the lasting value of the enterprise.

The challenge of effectively changing the value-creating work proceeds best when we pay mindful attention to some key principles. After all, we are talking about changing the work of *people* ... people who we have been asking to perform work in one way, and now we are asking them to change. As Lynn described in the process introduced at UP, nowhere in a change process is it more critical to be mindful of the what, the why, and the how of making change. Here, as always, some key questions and guiding principles show us a way forward:

- What is the value being created by the work?
- How can work be done with needed quality, minimum waste, and maximum safety?
- What unnecessary steps can be eliminated?
- What struggles can be alleviated from the person doing the work?
- How can the work be designed with just the right level of challenge and structured to make it easy to learn and improve?

Eliminating waste and its sources is a great way to ensure that all the work we are asking people to do is *meaningful* and that each bit adds value to the product or service we are providing. Standardizing work combined with establishing structured approaches to problem solving, improvement, as well as innovation that may be continuous or discontinuous, enables each member of the organization to contribute their best.

Our aim should be to never waste the time and effort of the individuals who spend most of their waking lives creating value on behalf of our customers. And, as a change leader, you will find no greater joy in your work than alleviating the needless burden from the work of someone doing their best to create value.

Summary

In this section, we discussed the nuts and bolts of the Change Initiative. This is where you and your team will ensure that you thoroughly understand the context in which the change will take place and the existing work processes that are already in place. Your team will work with subject-matter experts and employees to design the new work that will be done to enact the change. You will also want to discuss ways to try or experiment with the initiative before the full launch. This step is not complete until your team creates the measurements that will be used for continuously improving the initiative, including employee feedback loops to gain buy-in.

YOUR TURN

Refer to the guide *at the end of this book when you are ready to work through the design, do, and improve element of the Change Questions process. The digital workbook contains many of the forms shown in this chapter in a fillable PDF format.*

Engage and Develop Employees

Figure 4.1: Change Questions Diagram - Engage & Develop

*I*n the last chapter, I shared how our change team began to identify where the learning trials would take place. The change team was very surprised when I advocated using the 20-60-20 model to finalize the learning trial location. This is a method that isn't often considered, but as you will see in this chapter, it is extremely effective because it

Lynn's
S T O R Y

harnesses the power of change agents to engage employees. Employee engagement is essential to the sustainment of any Change Initiative.

We've discussed the importance of defining the purpose of the Change Initiative and the value that you expect to get from it. We've covered critical aspects of designing the work, planning how to do the work on a trial basis, and how to measure the value of the change and improve the work following the PDCA cycle. These steps are critical, but you can't complete them without truly engaged employees who have developed the capability to do the value-creating work.

In this chapter, we will present various methods of building employee engagement including consistent and frequent communication and recognition for employees who successfully implement the change. We will also discuss some basic principles and methods for building needed capabilities. Being intentional about capability development will help you build your team's skills and remove obstacles ahead of a successful launch.

EMPLOYEE ENGAGEMENT—WHAT TO DO

Resistance to Change – It's a Big Deal

What is Isaac Newton's first law? It's inertia. What is inertia? It's a law of physics that says if a body is at rest or moving at a constant speed, it will continue in its present state unless it is acted upon by a force. In other words, the status quo will prevail unless a force changes it. Further studies have explicitly identified a natural bias toward the status quo vs. change in the non-physical, social-economic world as well.

Resistance to change is common knowledge today, even as it was in the days of Machiavelli (1469-1527) and Newton (1643-1727). **Yet, we**

often implement sweeping organizational change without even considering how to handle the natural resistance to the change. How can this be, given all the research showing that it's a big deal?

One of the foundational models for change didn't come from the field of organizational change, but rather from the study of individuals trying to change their behaviors for the benefit of their own families. You see, the developer of this early change model, Virginia Satir, was a psychotherapist who was given the honorific title of Mother of Family Therapy. In the 1960s, she introduced the Satir Change Model, which originated from her research of working with troubled families.

She published her popular model in 1991 which was subsequently incorporated into research relating to organizational change in the 1990s and 2000s. One of the key points of Satir's model is that resistance is inevitable. Therefore, it is important to anticipate it and prepare solutions for resistance in advance, which is also one of the key messages behind the Change Questions. Satir advocated that creating a listening framework and support system for those involved in the change will help overcome resistance to the change.

In our own experience leading change, we have found that there can be positive outcomes by engaging the people who are resistant to change if we approach them with genuine respect rather than fear, distrust, or disdain. Unsurprisingly, the early research on change agents and resisters promoted the idea that change agents were the good folks who were trying to open the eyes of the uninitiated, while those negative to change were intent on messing things up for the organization.

Several studies tackled this change-agent-centric bias head-on by focusing on the positive outcomes that can be obtained from actively involving those who are resistant to the change. The authors found that "resistance" may be the misperception applied by the change agent to those who are rationally seeking clarification regarding the change.

The way change agents frame their perceptions of the people who offer objections to the change is key. If change agents can view the negative feedback they receive as legitimate concerns from people who really care and feel strongly about their work, the relationship will be more likely to proceed on a path of mutual respect and create better dialogue. (Recall Lynn's experience at UP when she mislabeled someone who resisted her suggested change as negative, when in fact, the person was seeking clarity and became one of the greatest supporters of the change once he felt understood and respected.)

In many cases, you can use resistance to help your Change Initiative succeed by addressing people's concerns and legitimizing their feedback, both negative and positive. When individuals feel that their concerns are respected and addressed, they are much more likely to support the change, which can lead to a domino effect.

You may eventually find that it is advisable to have a strategy for all three groups in the 20-60-20 change model—change agents, those who are neutral, and resistors. It is also useful to note that 20-60-20 is just a model. The actual situation will be more nuanced and may vary across organizations depending upon the orientation of different hiring managers (i.e., leaders who are comfortable with change may be more likely to hire employees who are comfortable with change, and people who are uncomfortable with change are less likely to want to stay in a department that is frequently changing). Later in this chapter, we discuss how to create the communication and recognition necessary to successfully spread your change to the entire organization, especially the neutral 60 percent within the curve.

Engaging employees is not an isolated event, nor are the actions you take to engage employees limited to the areas we cover in this chapter. There are multiple opportunities to engage employees throughout all of the Change Initiative activities. For example, your change team may seek employee feedback within the progress checks and as you design the new work to be done. The way that your team handles this feedback may serve to engage or even disengage the employees. For the remainder of this chapter, we will focus on specific actions, tools, and methods that you and your change team can use to work with resistance in a positive way and engage employees in the change.

Change Initiative Facilitators

If your initiative requires the use of facilitators (people who assist in launching the change), you will want to choose individuals who are skilled in engaging others to explore new ideas and ways of working. Here are some foundational attributes to look for:

Respect for People

- There should be a recognition that the people who are doing the work are skilled, have good ideas, and care about doing a good job. A know-it-all facilitator is rarely successful.

Give People a Voice in the Change

- A "fully-baked" solution or change will generally be less successful than letting employees give input into various elements of the change. In addition, once the change has been implemented, a really good facilitator gives all the credit to the team. This person knows the change isn't possible without the full strength of the team.

Good Communication and Listening Skills

- Communicating often and through multiple modes in a manner that is respectful and approachable is essential. Not only does this help your Change Initiative become successful, but it also helps people feel connected to each other with a larger sense of purpose. It's important to regularly ask for feedback and be open to suggestions without reacting to them negatively.

Ability to Compromise

- Some facilitators approach change work believing they have their "marching orders from above" to facilitate change according to a formula with no room for deviation. Compromise is almost always important because the perfect initiative that isn't sustained due to lack of buy-in is never as good as the good-but-not-perfect initiative that is sustained.

Consensus Building

- Many times, there are conflicting voices in the room. A good facilitator will make sure everyone feels heard and work toward facilitating the group to an agreement.

Passion

- All the previous attributes tend to motivate people to engage in the change. An additional attribute that helps to motivate people is authentic passion—not the fake rah-rah passion, but real passion and belief in the initiative. Along with that, frequent praise and celebration of team successes go a long way.

BUILDING CAPABILITY—WHAT TO DO

Capability Building Overview

When your change team specified the new work to be done in chapter 3, Design, Do, and Improve the Work, you should have started considering which capabilities will enable your organization's employees to implement the change. We often think of capability building as limited to training and development, but we have found that a broader definition of capability building is necessary.

Have you ever been in an organization where employees were asked to implement a change, only to find that the mechanisms for implementing the change were not in place, or (even worse) the existing mechanisms worked against the new change? For example, employees in a call center may be given the new directive of "go the extra mile to solve customer problems." Let's assume that they have been trained on how to go the extra mile, as a matter of capability. However, if their call performance was still measured by the time it took to handle a customer call, employees might find that going the extra mile would result in spending more time on the call, negatively impacting their performance metric. Or, what about when people are asked to make a change to the way they do their tasks, only to discover that the new software to be used in the change doesn't work? These are common obstacles that prevent willing people from implementing change. Bottom line: if the old way of doing things works against the new way, the old way will win.

In a multi-industry study, it was found that employee *capability* has a much greater impact on people's performance during the Change Initiative than even employee *commitment* (buy-in) to the initiative.

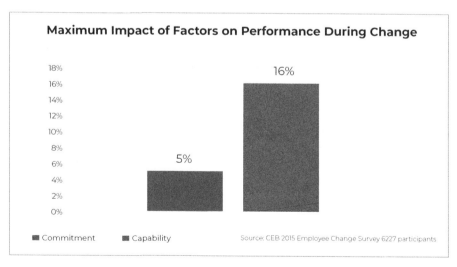

Figure 4.2: Maximum Impact of Factors on Performance During Change

> **"After changes occur, employees often find that underlying structures, processes, and rules have not kept pace. The infrastructure that previously supported employees, if unmodified, may now hinder employees' ability to adapt. They may no longer know how to get their work done or even what they should be doing. Employees struggle to identify who can help them or whom they need to work with."**
>
> - CEB EMPLOYEE CHANGE STUDY, 2015

A follow-up study on resources needed during Change Initiatives determined that "...information, tools, training, peers, and internal subject-matter experts are the raw materials that employees need in the new work environment ...".

Research has also shown that people who believe they have been treated fairly are more likely to develop positive behaviors associated with change. "Unfair" perceptions often happen when there is a redistribution of resources, or processes and procedures are changed in a way that is perceived as unfair to the individuals in question.

We have summarized capability building into three areas and will provide examples of each later in this chapter:

- Tools,
- Resources,
- Training and Development.

We will discuss an additional area, infrastructure, in the next chapter.

When people have adequate tools, resources, and training, they can turn their openness and willingness to change into the *capabilities* they need to enact change.

Change Question

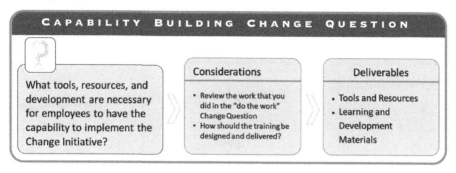

Figure 4.3: Capability Building Change Question

You will likely need to include at least some of the following individuals in your capability building activities:

- Process/subject-matter experts in the location where the change will take place,
- Employees who do the work where the change will take place,
- Union representatives (if any),
- Learning and development experts.

In this step of the Change Questions process, your team will reflect upon the information that you have gathered so far and take steps to fill the knowledge gaps in the key obstacle areas of tools, resources, and training. For example, in the last chapter, you created a design of the new work. In this portion of the process, you may need to gather additional information by observing specific work processes, talking directly with employees doing the work, or reviewing existing training materials. Once you feel comfortable with your work design, you can proceed to this step of developing the tools, resources, and training materials to support the new work.

An easy way to spark meaningful discussion around the capability building areas is to imagine each of the employee target groups in light of the questions listed in columns 2-4 in the following form.

Capability Building Worksheet

Employee Target Group	What Tools are Needed?	What Resources are Needed?	What Training and Development are Needed?

Figure 4.4: Capability Building Worksheet

Definitions:

Tools: The device, forms, or equipment needed to carry out a particular function. Tools can be electronic or non-electronic, hardware or software, and can be found in all environments.

Resources: Materials, budget, staff, mentors, and other aids necessary for effective operation.

Training and Development: The activities of building employee capabilities in a particular skill or type of behavior.

Next Steps

When you have completed the capability building form there may be specific actions needed. The first two items, tools and resources, require different actions than training and development. The first two items will often require guidance, ownership, and approval from the departments involved. A sure path to employee resistance is to create new tools and resources *without* input and approval from the departments that own those areas. We can't emphasize this enough! Create real partnerships in the areas where the change will take place by actively engaging leadership and employees in the design and approval of the enabling items.

Training and development will be most effective if guided by an expert on the subject. If your organization has a learning and development department or has access to experts who are skilled in developing people, then ideally it is those individuals who will lead the creation of the training and development materials and process. The days of a "trainer" standing in the front of the classroom and dryly reading every word of every slide are over. The quality of the development, training delivery, coaching, and training materials can have a huge impact on the success of your initiative.

Here are some good principles and practices for training:

1. **On-the-job training and development (OJT, OJD):** OJT/OJD occurs when people are developed in the place where the actual work takes place. This method pairs experience with knowledge, helps people learn the work through doing the work, and ensures the real-world fit between the new work and work location realities. It often shortens the learning curve and helps people learn the work through actually doing the work.

2. **A variety of classroom teaching techniques:** According to many studies, the average attention span of an adult learner is approximately twenty minutes. Using this as a guideline, it is often helpful to change learning activities every twenty minutes or so. For example, the training can rotate through things like lectures, Q&As, hands-on activities, break-out groups, experiments, case-study work, and active classroom sharing.

3. **A variety of visual aid materials:** The instructor can hold interest and create better learning opportunities by using a variety of visual instructional materials such as slides, whiteboards, flip-charts, and physical demonstration objects.

4. **Real-world stories:** Stories work well when paired with a learning point to demonstrate how the lesson translates into real-life situations. These stories also help to maintain team members' interest and assist them in remembering key points.

5. **Check for retention and solicit feedback:** The feedback-retention loop occurs when the trainer or coach asks frequent questions to check for understanding.

6. **Offer peer-to-peer and collaborative learning opportunities:** The training can offer opportunities for people to share their experiences and collaborate on projects related to the subject.

7. **Multiple delivery methods:** People have different learning styles. If you can offer several delivery methods such as online, gamification, videos, in-class instruction, and hands-on learning, you can maximize your training impact across a variety of learning styles.

You probably won't be able to cover all of these good practices, but you can use this list as a reference while your team develops its training programs to incorporate as many good practices as appropriate for your organization.

BUILDING CAPABILITY—HOW TO DO IT

Capability Building

The UP change team brainstormed the necessary tools, resources, and development/training needed for its successful adoption. The core membership of the change team included representatives from four of the five operating departments, which helped to supply subject-matter expertise in

many of these areas. The change team also included a team member who was certified in training and development.

In this partial example outlined in Figure 4.5, the change team identified both unionized and non-unionized employees who were participating in the learning trials as target groups. This is shown in the first column of the second row. In the second row, the team identified the top leadership as another target group. This form was also completed for several other groups (not shown).

UP Way Capability Building Worksheet

Target Group	What Tools are Needed?	What Resources are Needed?	What Training and Development are Needed?
All non-union employees and targeted union employees in learning trials.	■ Leader standard work (LSW) template forms ■ Standard work forms ■ Standard work portal	■ Help-line ■ Mentoring support	Classroom & on the job delivery: ■ UP Way overview ■ 5S & visual management ■ Leader standard work ■ Standard work ■ Value stream mapping ■ Problem solving ■ Standard work portal
Executive leadership	■ FAQs to answer employee questions ■ LSW template forms ■ Standard work forms ■ Standard work portal	■ Key messages ■ Mentoring support	■ Executive UP Way overview ■ All training listed above

Figure 4.5: UP Way Capability Building Worksheet

Tools: *Both groups needed the same tools such as new forms and an online portal for standard work to reside, as well as additional tools specific to their group.*

Resources: *The CI department staffed a help-line where people could get their questions answered. In addition, as the change was introduced, each targeted area was assigned an on-site individual who mentored those who were actively involved in the UP Way. The executive leadership members were given a list of key messages for consistent communication with their employees.*

Training and Development: *The change team determined that much of the training would be identical. However, the leadership group would also get a high-level overview for its use in introducing the change to others. The delivery method was determined to be classroom or on-the-job.*

After the change team completed this form, we assigned various team members to validate our assumptions and perform observations in key areas to ensure that we had an accurate understanding of the obstacles we needed to remove. We invited subject-matter experts to our change team meetings and asked for feedback and input into our plan as we met with the departments that would be affected by the change.

We gave people inside and outside of the change team specific responsibilities to develop the tools to remove the obstacles. For example, we paired a CI specialist with an IT specialist to build the standard work portal. Neither of them was a member of the change team; however, given the magnitude of items we had to design and build, we knew we needed to reach far and wide in engaging people to assist us. We were able to test many of these new training modules, tools, resources, structures, and processes within the learning trials and continued to make significant improvements as we went along.

COMMUNICATION—WHAT TO DO, PART 1

Communication is critical to the success of a Change Initiative. In a global study across multiple industries, respondents were given twenty-four possible areas to reflect upon regarding their most recent Change Initiative. The respondents chose "communication" as the key area for successful implementation of change. There are many published models for how to implement successful change. The one thing that most of these models have in common is the importance of effectively communicating the purpose of the initiative. In an influential article, John Kotter advocates the need to create a vision and to communicate the vision using "every vehicle possible." Kotter advised that communication is an essential factor in his change model.

Change Question

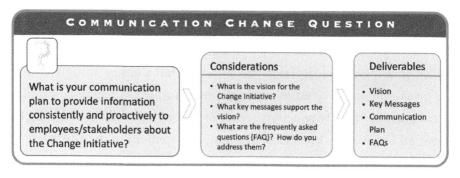

Figure 4.6: Communication Change Question

The more you engage and effectively communicate with employees, the greater the likelihood that your Change Initiative will sustain. Yet—many teams initiate a major change without considering such important factors as how to communicate the change, how to give positive reinforcement to the change, and how to recognize the employees that have successfully adopted the change.

We have found it helpful to work through a comprehensive communication strategy that includes the following elements:

- Vision statement,
- Key messages,
- Communication plan,
- FAQs, and
- Recognition.

This process will benefit from the input of specialists in these areas:

- Communications
- Human Resources

The Vision Statement

The foundation of your communication plan is the vision statement. This is a compelling, concise, and aspirational statement that describes the future state of the successful change. An inspiring vision will assist in guiding behavior and help the organization achieve its goals.

In chapter 2, we covered the development of the purpose statement, which is a high-level description of the overall Change Initiative. The vision statement is typically more detailed and may include additional areas such as how, why, where, who, or when. You will not be able to cover all these areas in one concise vision statement without it becoming cumbersome and lengthy. Instead, determine the two or three most important items to include.

Some guidelines to keep in mind when writing the vision statement include:

- Keep it brief by including only the most important points.
- Make it aspirational.
- Check for clarity of goal.
- Try to obtain a first draft quickly in hours not days.

A note on the last point: There is a delicate balance between taking the time to write a good vision statement and losing momentum while wordsmithing a vision statement to the nth degree. We share one example of a method to quickly get to a final version of a strong vision statement in the UP Way story later in this chapter.

Key Messages

The purpose of the key messages is to have consistent communication around the critical aspects of your initiative. Think of key messages as talking points that you and your team can provide to leaders throughout the organization and touch points to be used in written change-related communications disseminated both internally and externally. Unfortunately, senior executives are often expected to "wing it" when communicating about the change. It's a bit like the telephone game where the message changes each time it's passed from person to person until it's unrecognizable.

One study found that when leaders used a consistent change story it increased the probability that the change would be successful. When initiating change, consistent and repeated messages are essential. Consider as a rule of thumb that an optimum number of key messages may be two or three for a simple change and up to ten for a complex change.

Most people are familiar with the WIIFM acronym for What's In It For Me. In addition to letting people know how they will personally benefit from the change, employees also want to know WHY it's important for the change to take place. Your team will want to include both important points in your key messages.

When you develop your communication plan you be guided to target key messages to specific audiences. These key messages can be used in the communication plan to describe the change through vehicles such as speeches, town halls, social media, small group meetings, emails, website copy, and company publications. Examples of key messages are:

■ The company has been losing market share. The new sales and marketing program will help us reach more customers and increase our market share.

■ The organization's travel costs are rising. The new travel booking website will help lower our costs while making booking travel easier for employees.

You will find the key message worksheet for your team's use in the digital workbook.

Key Messages Worksheet

#	What are the key messages that support the Change Initiative?
1.	
2.	
3.	
4.	
5.	

Figure 4.7: Key Messages Worksheet

The Communication Plan

The communication plan brings together the vision statement, key messages, and other aspects of the change such as success stories, implementation timeframes, and lessons learned. These elements are paired with target audiences and given communication timelines. A solid communication plan will typically include the following elements:

1. Theme: What is the theme of the communication?
2. Key Message (from the key messages worksheet): What key message does the theme support?
3. Target Audience: Who is the recipient of the message?

4. Method/Publication: What is the delivery method of the communication?

5. Date(s): When will the communication be delivered?

6. Responsible: Who will be responsible for delivering the communication?

Communication Plan Worksheet

Theme	Key Message (#)	Target Audience	Method/ Publication	Date(s)	Responsible

Figure 4.8: Communication Plan Worksheet

COMMUNICATION—HOW TO DO IT, PART 1

Vision Statement, Key Messages, and Communication Plan

Lynn's STORY

*T*he change team got together to write the vision statement, which flowed from the purpose statement. Even though we had previously agreed on the purpose statement, which had been guided by and approved by our leadership, I was not certain that we were completely aligned on the vision. We had been using the G.R.P.I. (Goals, Roles, Process, and Interpersonal) tool each week and we were moving closer to alignment, but we still were not totally in agreement on key areas of the G.R.P.I. I was concerned about creating the vision statement because I felt that we still had different views of what the vision would be. In addition, only one *of the team members had any experience with Lean, so most of them couldn't conceive of what Lean at UP might even look like.*

I decided to use the fifteen-word tool to help streamline the process of creating the vision statement. These are the steps:

1. *Ask participants to write their idea of the vision statement in fifteen words or less. Give them 20 minutes to do so.*

2. *Tape or copy everyone's fifteen-word vision statement onto a whiteboard or wall.*

3. *Identify/circle the words that are common across most of the vision statements.*

4. *Use the common words to work toward gaining consensus on the keywords to be included in the final vision statement.*

After completing this activity, we had a rough draft of a vision statement. It was longer than I wanted because the team members couldn't agree on the top priorities, but we had something to start circulating to leadership. After input from leadership, we were able to finalize the vision statement.

UP Way Vision Statement

The UP Way engages all employees to continuously improve safety, service, and productivity by utilizing methods to standardize work, eliminate variability, and solve problems at their root cause, resulting in greater employee and customer satisfaction.

The team had a much easier time developing the key messages. The team members had been interacting with their leaders and colleagues in the various operating departments and knew what the issues were and what the UP Way was intended to do. We created ten key messages that were important to highlight when discussing UP Way. The messages are numbered for ease of reference in the communication plan.

UP Way Key Messages (Partial List)

The UP Way:

1. *Aims to grow the business, not decrease the workforce. Operational efficiencies achieved through UP Way will enable UP to grow and hire.*
2. *Creates a "way to lead" that engages employees and promotes trust, respect, and teamwork.*
3. *Promotes "forest rangers" instead of "firefighters," transitioning UP to an organization that uses proactive processes to deliver consistent results.*
4. *Is not the flavor of the month.*

The change team used the communications plan format to bring together the strategies to introduce and support the UP Way, as shown in the partial listing of the communication plan.

UP Way Communication Plan Worksheet

Theme	Key Message (#)	Target Audience	Method/ Publication	Date(s)	Responsible
Highlight early success stories in UP Way deployment.	#6	All UP employees	Article in UP Online	Beginning Jan – then monthly	Emma Grace, communications department
Introduce UP Way vision and give overview of program.	#1, 4 & 8	All UP employees	All speeches from CEO that are internal to UP	Beginning Oct – then ongoing	CEO with Emma Grace
Overview of program with timeline.	#1, 4 & 8	Learning trial location's employees	Email from department I& CI leader	Oct.	Department leader

Figure 4.9: UP Way Communication Plan Worksheet

Our change team benefited greatly by including Emma Grace, a communications specialist during this process. One of the suggestions she made was to encapsulate many of these key messages within a graphic. Fortunately, UP's Communication Department included a graphic designer, who created the UP Way logo. This image was used in multiple ways. It quickly became recognizable by everyone in the organization and helped to reinforce the UP Way.

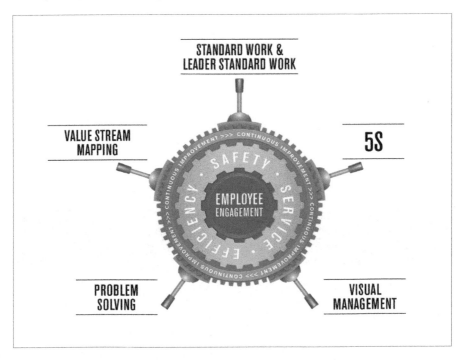

Figure 4.10: UP Way Logo

You can see that UP placed employee engagement at the very center of these five UP Way elements (shown in the spokes). A key concept of the UP Way is that the employees who do the day-to-day work are engaged and empowered to improve their processes. UP surrounded the employee engagement center with three of the expected values of doing UP Way: improve safety, improve service to customers and stakeholders, and improve efficiency. The tools used to accomplish all these goals are on the spokes: standard work and leader standard work, 5S workplace organization, visual management, value stream mapping, and problem solving.

COMMUNICATION—WHAT TO DO, PART 2

Frequently Asked Questions (FAQs)

Every major Change Initiative inevitably generates questions from diverse groups of people with multiple viewpoints. For example, people often want to know if the change will affect their pay or the way they perform their daily work. Rather than leave individual managers with the responsibility to answer these difficult questions—and perhaps come up with contradictory answers—we strongly recommend that your change team generate a list of these anticipated questions in advance, along with the appropriate answers.

Several burning questions that people generally have about any given Change Initiative are:

- What will happen to *me* in the Change Initiative?
- What is in it for me if this change takes place?
- What support/resources will I have to make this change?
- Why would I want to participate in the change?
- Is it possible that I will lose my job if this change results in fewer employees needed to do the work?
- What will be the impact on the company, customers, and stakeholders?
- What is the timing of the change?

Do you really want managers to *guess* at the answers to these types of questions?

An easy and effective way to generate a useful list of FAQs is to ask team members to keep track of the questions they receive regarding the change. In early discussions before the change is implemented, people often ask, "So, how does this change affect X?"

Some of your FAQs will cover difficult ground. In fact, at UP, we had to work through some of the answers with the legal and human resources departments. Any organization with union employees will most likely have to review decisions that arise from FAQs with union representation. Again, answers to the most difficult questions may derail your initiative if people have no option but to guess at the answer and give incorrect information. We challenge you and your team to wrestle through the most difficult questions in advance.

Some of the resources you need to obtain accurate responses to FAQs may be outside of your working group. If so, you can assign individuals in your team to meet with the appropriate parties to get more information and craft responses. We generally recommend that you obtain approval from top leadership on responses, especially to the most difficult or sensitive questions or answers where leadership guidance is necessary.

Once you develop your FAQs and gain approval from critical parties, you can distribute them to leaders at all levels within your organization and publish or post them in an easily accessible location for all employees to view.

COMMUNICATION—HOW TO DO IT, PART 2

UP Way FAQs

*W*hile serving on the change team, our team members gathered many questions about the UP Way from their colleagues. They heard concerns and reasons why people thought it wouldn't work. We were able to compile a robust FAQ list, as follows:

UP FAQs (Partial List)

1. *Will employee non-adherence or non-participation in the UP Way lead to disciplinary actions for union employees?*

2. *How will UP Way implementation be incorporated into performance evaluations?*

3. *If a work group reduces the time it takes to perform a process, will the workforce be reduced?*

We reached out to experts (legal, human resources, and union leadership) for input into the questions we could not answer. Once we had answers to all the FAQs, we obtained leadership approval. We distributed the FAQs to all UP managers. We then posted them on UP's employee website where they were available to all employees.

RECOGNITION—WHAT TO DO

Change Question

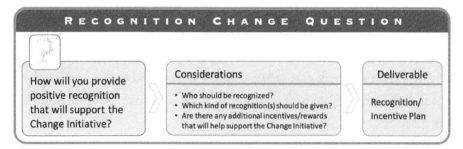

Figure 4.11: Recognition Change Question

Recognition Overview

Companies with recognition-rich cultures generally outperform companies that do not focus on recognition. Best practices around recognition include giving recognition frequently and openly. This section will help your team think about ways to recognize employees frequently and openly.

During the ten years that Doug Conant led Campbell's Soup Company, he was credited with transforming the company by increasing employee morale and delivering strong financial performance. During multiple interviews where he was asked how he achieved these results, Conant pointed to the primary driver: saying thank you. During his ten-year tenure, he wrote 30,000 thank-you notes to employees. Each day he dedicated an hour of his time to writing ten to twenty thank-you notes to employees at all levels of the organization.

Notice that saying thank you is a recognition rather than a material reward. People often dismiss the impact of recognition because they think people won't respond to recognition alone. However, recognition is incredibly powerful all on its own. In this section, we focus on recognition. If your organization chooses to also provide rewards or incentives to reinforce positive behavior and outcomes, you can use this same format. We have discovered, however, that recognition delivers such powerful results, rewards are often secondary.

Many Change Initiatives are implemented without advance thought about how to positively reinforce any early successes. Often, it's only when organizations have a few successes racked up, that they begin to think about how to publicize those successes. We recommend having an advance plan that will gather the success stories and communicate them throughout the whole organization as soon as those accomplishments are discernible.

Recognition Provides Motivation for the Neutral Group

When you actively recognize the early successes within the initiative, you not only inspire the change agents or the teams being recognized, but also motivate the middle 60 percent of people who are neutral to the change. For your Change Initiative to succeed, you must be able to move the implementation from the early adapters to the neutral middle majority to create the tipping point needed to ensure the change takes hold and sustains. Recognition helps to counterbalance the persuading drumbeat of negative feedback that will also seek to influence the neutral 60 percent.

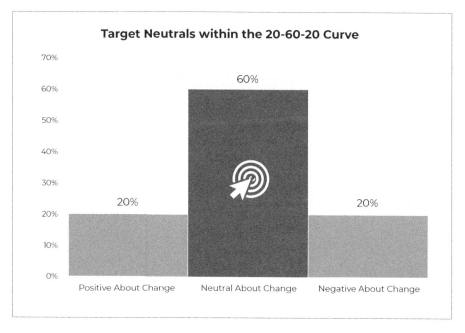

Figure 4.12: Target Neutrals Within the 20-60-20 Curve

Using the form within the Change Questions, your team will determine:

1. Who will be recognized,
2. What method will be used to recognize the success,
3. Who the audience is for the recognition, and
4. Who will give the recognition.

The Change Questions in this section will also prompt you to think about possible incentives and rewards that will help move the initiative forward.

Recognition Worksheet

Who will be recognized?	Where/what is recognition?	Is there an audience for the recognition?	Additional details	Who will implement/ give the recognition?

Figure 4.13: Recognition Worksheet

RECOGNITION—HOW TO DO IT

Employee Recognition

*O*ur change team decided to incorporate recognition into as many existing Operating Department activities as possible. For example, each year the department held a leadership conference, where the top 100 operating leaders gathered. The change team decided that we would film UP Way success stories and show them at the annual leadership conference. The department also held a monthly staff meeting. We agreed that we would feature a presentation by a team who had a success story relating to UP Way on a regular basis at the staff meetings.

Many additional recognition activities were developed using the company-wide monthly publication, website, and other vehicles. The change team designated that incentives and rewards would be handled at the local level. We encouraged service units to create localized t-shirts, pins, medallions, etc., to distribute to team members as appropriate.

UP Way Recognition Worksheet

Who will be recognized?	Where/what is recognition?	Is there an audience for the recognition?	Additional details	Who will implement/ give the recognition?
Teams that have successfully implemented elements of the UP Way	Featured on videos at the Leadership Conference	First, the top 200 leaders of the company & afterwards all employees	Videos will be placed on the UP website after conference for wide viewing	Departmental leaders will nominate teams
Projects teams with good results	Presentation at Operating Staff Meeting	Operating leadership	Each month 1 project team will report-out	Alternate N, S, W Regions

Partial Listing

Figure 4.14: UP Way Recognition Worksheet

Practical Application: Engage and Develop Employees

Most car owners know that their vehicles should be serviced regularly and often struggle to complete the service in a timely manner. Many car companies recommend that the routine service should happen every 5,000 – 10,000 miles, and for a lot of us, that milestone seems to come up much too quickly. Locomotives should also be serviced for routine maintenance regularly. It is often a challenge to pull a locomotive off a busy track within the service window and do a quick turnaround so it can get right back to the job of pulling freight across the country with as few breakdowns as possible.

UP's freight volume was steadily growing, so we needed to correspondingly increase the number of locomotives that could be serviced in our various locomotive shops around our system. Casey, a leader at one of the shops, offered to host the learning trial for the UP Way at her location, specifically targeted at increasing velocity through the servicing area. The union shop had not been introduced to the UP Way, so she started by working with the local union leadership. Casey described the servicing challenge, sought input from the people who did the work, and discussed the potential benefits they would see if changes could be made.

After the initial conversation, Casey organized a benchmarking trip with the union leaders to observe a unionized manufacturing process that had implemented Lean. The facility was doing things like workplace organization, visual management, standard work, and problem solving. The employees in this workplace described the changes that were made in the way that they did their work as well as the changes that the union made to be able to support the new work. The enthusiasm of the employees at this company was evident, and to the great credit of UP's union leadership, they were willing to give it a try.

As the team worked through the enabling items necessary to allow the new work to begin, they realized that new roles and responsibilities would have to be written for each job, and then the jobs would have to be reposted. This was a heck of a lot of work, but it was essential. The team also had to build new capabilities and began to develop people in the UP Way through training, benchmarking, and mentoring. One of the goals was to transition the servicing line of the locomotive shop from management-led scheduling of the work to having the union employees run the line themselves. The active managers were moved to other jobs within the shop and implemented a paging system for the union employees to call a manager if they had a problem they couldn't solve.

It didn't stop there. The communication plan involved a monthly letter to be sent to all the locomotive shops from Casey's manager, Tyrone, to highlight the progress of the UP Way learning trial at the locomotive shop. Tyrone's weekly calls with the locomotive shop leaders also recognized the activities and successful results of the learning trial. Slowly, other locomotive shops became interested in the activities of the learning trial and made benchmarking visits to learn what had happened. The visits were hosted by the union employees who were proud to show their peers what they had done. Several other locomotive shops followed suit and the UP Way spread to more locations.

After just one month of operating in this new way of doing things, Casey saw a 27 percent increase in the number of locomotives serviced in the learning trial location. The increased volume was sustained at the learning trial location and spread to others around the system. We also saw the engagement of the employees increase dramatically, which was demonstrated by the willing involvement of the employees to participate in problem solving activities which led to additional workplace improvements.

Climbing a mountain may begin with deciding to climb the mountain—and gearing oneself up with the passion to do the necessary preparation—but in the end, success will only come if one develops the capability to ... climb a mountain. Strength, stamina, and climbing technique will all be required.

Interestingly, many change or kaizen efforts (kaizen is simply the spirit and process of an organization continually improving itself to meet its purpose at all levels) take basic capabilities for granted, presuming that the mundane techniques required to do the work are fully embedded or easily learned, deep down in the bowels of the organization. You can sometimes hear the ship's captain (to switch metaphors) screaming down to the technicians in the engine room, "I need more power – now!" Meanwhile, the technicians don't actually know how to get any more horsepower out of the only engines they have been given to work with.

If we want people to contribute more, what can we as an organization do to help them do so? Do we view people as commodities with skills to buy and sell or as valued sources of lasting competitive advantage?

Lynn describes the skills (and work) required of a Change Initiative leadership team, leveraging her experience with the team at UP and elsewhere. Facilitation skills, communication skills (and plan), and general "people skills." Meanwhile, down in the engine room, the technicians need new skills, too; skills to do the work differently to get more power out of their engines, as well as enhanced problem-solving skills to cope with long-standing problems or situations they have never faced before. Lean practitioners have long held to a view that stems from the earliest days of Toyota, but that also finds theoretical foundation going back at least as far as John Dewey who argued that "learning" and "doing" should not and, in fact, cannot be separated.

"Learn through doing" is the common catchphrase, which sounds so simple as to be trite. In fact, establishing processes whereby *those doing the work can learn as they do it* requires (as do most things of value in life) significant attention and effort. This old idea finds modern expression in the "execution as learning" model of Harvard's Amy Edmonson. Work is best *designed* so that it provides natural feedback, and people need to be developed (as in, coached, mentored, and given room to grow) so that they know how to identify and use that feedback.

That's the double-loop of the PDCA cycle of learning introduced in chapter 3. And it's the way forward to achieving what is arguably— per Taka Fujimoto, Japan's foremost Lean thinker in academia—the most important capability of all, which is the "capability for capability development" which can also be thought of as an organization's evolutionary capability. Since circumstances in business are changing at such seemingly increasingly rapid rates, capability requirements will change accordingly. The most successful organizations will be those that develop this dynamic capability development capability. So, capabilities come in different shapes and sizes. Purely individual technical capability is one thing, organizational capability to improve is quite another. And wherever we are asking our organization (and expecting ourselves) to learn willingly and to exert discretionary effort, it behooves us to be cognizant of the social environment within which we all work.

As we provide to each employee work that meaningfully contributes directly to the value that the organization creates for customers—ensuring that employees know that they are the *owner* of the outcome of the work they are performing—this creates the conditions for each person to find fulfillment and to actively seek greater engagement. The best way we can show respect for the members of our organization is to allow them to be the owner of the outcome of his or her work. From there, we can nurture yet challenge, and challenge yet encourage, so individuals have opportunities to grow as they contribute to the mission of the enterprise.

It is confidence-inspiring to know that, using these insights, principles, and practices, we can willfully enhance our organization's chances of long-term success.

Summary

In this chapter, we focused entirely on engaging and developing employees through change agents, capability building, communication, and recognition. Your efforts in creating an inspiring vision will help to motivate employees. However, a strong vision alone is not enough; people will have questions that can be readily answered in the key messages and well-distributed FAQs. Your recognition plan will help identify successes so that you can publicize them through multiple channels. All of this can be wrapped up and pulled together in a cadence outlined in your communication plan, which you can then incorporate in your overall iterative implementation plan (to be covered in Chapter 7).

YOUR TURN

Refer to the guide at the end of this book when you are ready to work through the engage and develop element of the Change Questions. The digital workbook contains many of the forms shown in this chapter and are in a fillable PDF format.

Establish a Management System and Leadership Behaviors that Support the Change Initiative

Figure 5.1: Change Questions Diagram - Engage & Develop

*B*y the time our change team began to consider management system and leadership, I had only been at the company for a few months. I was now at the point in the Change Questions process where

I needed to understand how the leaders at UP led, and if there were things within UP's management system that would work against this massive initiative that touched all aspects of the Operating Department. I was forming relationships with my peers but was nowhere near the place where I could have open and honest conversations with all of them regarding the less-than-lovely areas within their leadership world. I also had to tread lightly within the change team so that I didn't appear to be a newbie from a different industry who was now going to tell everyone how to do their jobs. To quote the Wicked Witch of the West, "These things must be done delicately!"

In previous chapters, we touched briefly on the need to engage with specific leadership groups. This step focuses entirely on the management *system* of your organization and overall leadership support of your Change Initiative.

When introducing the Change Questions methodology, we often ask people to think about times when they have experienced a failed organizational change and to share reasons why they think it failed. One of the major reasons people give is "lack of leadership support." Their instincts aren't wrong. A quick online search of the lists that contain the top reasons why change efforts fail almost always include a reference to the lack of leadership support.

On the flip side, let's look at a study that researched why Change Initiatives succeeded. A study from 2015 found that 26 percent of the respondents said that the change they experienced was "very or completely successful." In reviewing the factors that were most critical to the successful change, the respondents said that the top two factors were communication and leadership involvement. The same study found that when leaders modeled the behavior identified in the initiative, it was five times more successful than initiatives where leadership did not model supportive behaviors.

Even in the most ideal situation where you have top leadership committed to the change, it is often the case that there are leaders who do not support the change. Oh yes, they may *say* they support it, but as one study described the source of the change failure, it's not whether leaders *say* they are committed to supporting the change; it's whether their *behavior* ultimately supports the change. We all have known leaders who say they support Change Initiatives, but their actions speak much louder than their words and disabuse anyone of that notion of support.

All leaders, whether they be VPs, directors, managers, supervisors, or team leaders, have a tremendous impact on team members, especially their direct reports. In addition to having support from top leadership, it is critical to have active, concrete behavioral support from *all* leaders at *all* levels of the organization to have successful change.

Change Questions

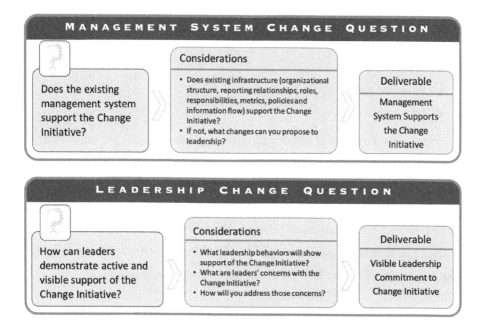

Figure 5.2: Management System and Leadership Change Questions

MANAGEMENT SYSTEM—WHAT TO DO

Overview

In chapter 4, Engage and Develop Employees, we considered how employees may be willing to make a change, but the existing *infrastructure* could prohibit them from doing so. The infrastructure we referred to is really your management system. It frames how activities are conducted to achieve the goals of your organization. These activities can include organizational structure, reporting relationships, roles and responsibilities, metrics, policies, information flow, and more.

Management System Definition: A system that frames how activities are conducted to achieve the goals of an organization.

Common Elements of a Management System:
- Organizational structure,
- Reporting relationships,
- Roles and responsibilities,
- Metrics,
- Policies, and
- Information flow.

Given the broad definition of a management system, your change team may find that there are many more elements of your system than the ones listed. In essence, your team will determine if there are any areas that will work against your initiative. If so, we suggest that you devise proposed solutions to enhance its adoption.

Here is a specific example of how to think about your management system, using only the common elements previously listed.

Example: Implementation of a New Online Billing System

Let's look at a department-specific Change Initiative by expanding on the new billing system example that we mentioned earlier. The initiative involved implementing a new online billing system that would increase billing accuracy.

- Organizational Structure:
  No change.

- Reporting Relationships:
  No change.

- Roles and Responsibilities:
  Create a new role of online troubleshooter/help desk. The billers' responsibilities will expand to include new system-related activities.

- Metrics:
  Retain the existing billing accuracy metric but apply it to electronic billing as well as any remaining manual billing activities.

- Policies:
  Create a streamlined policy relating to online approvals.

- Information Flow:
  The information flow will transition from being primarily manual to primarily electronic.

Management systems are inherently owned by the leadership in your organization. Because every Change Initiative and organization is different, there is no right answer regarding who will evaluate the management system in relation to the initiative. Your situation may call for leadership to complete the Change Question, your change team to complete the question, or a combination of both. In any case, final approval and ownership of the changes to the management system will be the responsibility of leadership in your group, department, or overall organization, depending upon the breadth of your Change Initiative.

Leadership Commitment and Behaviors

Visible, supportive behaviors by leadership are critical to the sustainment of any Change Initiative. You will find that some leaders are receptive to showing active support of the change and others are not. Ultimately, it is difficult to sustain an initiative if leaders are not willing to demonstrate outward support for the change. Unfortunately, in these cases, you and your change team may have to reconsider whether to pursue the change.

What are some supportive leadership behaviors?

- Leaders "walk the floor" where the Change Initiative is taking place and ask what is working and what isn't.
- Leaders actively participate in the change.
- Leaders seek solutions quickly when difficulties arise from the change.
- Leaders train employees in the change.
- Leaders regularly reinforce the vision, sharing the reasons for the change.
- Leaders regularly reinforce the expected benefits of the change.

The considerations in this section are:

- What leadership behaviors will show support of the Change Initiative?
- What are the leaders' concerns with the Change Initiative?
- How will you address those concerns?

In essence, a *catchball* process is often initiated with leadership where discussions occur and ideas are proposed, counter-proposed, and so on until there is an agreeable path forward. In other words—respectful, back-and-forth conversations occur to gain full leadership commitment to the initiative.

Catchball: the process of colleagues tossing ideas back and forth to improve them iteratively. In so doing, participants become informed of potential changes and have a chance to consider implications for themselves and the broader organization. —*Lean Thinkers, p.101, under Strategy Deployment.*

It may be that your situation is best suited for the catchball discussion to start with the leadership team generating the first answers to the questions. Or it may be that you and your change team start with idea or proposal generation, which is then reviewed with leadership for feedback. This is situational and only you and your change team will know the best path. Keep in mind, however, that most people don't like to be told what to do—even leadership! Tread lightly, humbly, and err on the side of over-communicating with leadership rather than under-communicating. It is better to bring a draft proposal for leadership feedback rather than a "fully baked plan."

How does all of this catchball work exactly? To get the feedback process started, you can use the form provided in the digital workbook to list leaders who are associated with the change. This form may include the leaders who are located where the learning trial will take place and can also include the leaders at the very top of the organization where the full implementation will occur after the learning trials. Often, this is an iterative process, in that the initial discussion may take place with one set of leaders, followed by cascading sets of leaders throughout the organization.

Names will be listed in the first column of the form (Figure 5.3). The person who is designated to discuss the topic with each leader will be listed in the second column (Discussion Owner).

Catchball Worksheet

Complete this at change team meeting		Complete this during meeting with leader	Complete this at next change team meeting	Complete this during discussion owner's next meeting with leader	
Leader	Discussion Owner	Leader's Concerns	Strategy to Address Concerns	Results	Agree?

Figure 5.3: Catchball Worksheet

The discussion owner will seek to understand the leader's concerns with the Change Initiative as well as views on the recommended changes. This will help you and your change team understand what obstacles should be removed or what changes should be made to gain full leadership commitment to the change.

In the feedback session with leadership, additional topics can be covered such as:

- How do you feel that you, as a leader, can best demonstrate visible support for the Change Initiative?

- What can the change team do to help support you in the adoption of the Change Initiative?

The discussion owner will then record the leader's concerns in the form's third column.

Once you gather this information, we suggest that your change team reconvene to review this information and handle it appropriately. This step may involve making revisions to the initiative, modifying a timeframe, revising the proposed leadership behaviors, or devising a specific solution/process change for one particular department or leader. It's impossible to know what to expect until you gather this information and truly take the time to reflect on it.

A note of caution: When your change team debriefs the information you obtained from leadership, confidentiality is necessary. We often humorously talk to the change team about invoking a "cone of silence" as in the 1960s TV show *Get Smart*. Right about here ... we planned to insert a very retro, fun, and dorky photo of the cone of silence, only to discover that we would have to pay many thousands of dollars for permission. So, if you aren't familiar with the cone of silence and want to bring a smile to your face, just google "The Crowded Cone of Silence." Yes—this was supposed to show advanced technology in the 1960s.

In other words, these sessions are confidential and usually limited to the change team members. Occasionally during the debriefing, some change team members will feel frustrated with leadership. You should obtain the agreement of confidentiality among the team members so that people can speak freely about their discussions with leadership and concerns. Your team will benefit from honest conversations in a trusting atmosphere. There is a fine line between descending into negativity and trashing certain leaders versus holding a constructive problem-solving session. Once leadership's concerns are well understood, you and your change team will want to discuss potential approaches and solutions for moving forward, rather than solely focus on a perceived lack of acceptance from certain leadership team members.

The change team's strategies to address each leader's concerns are recorded in the fourth column of the catchball worksheet. Instead of allowing leader ambivalence or even opposition to remain hidden and to fester, you can treat unsupportive stances as just another apparent obstacle to explore or a potential problem to solve. Or, to your surprise, you may find that the resistance arose from valid reasons! You've identified gaps between your ideas and reality. What can you and your team do to address those gaps?

The discussion owner can then have additional conversations with the leader and offer the change team's strategy to address the leader's concerns (catchball). The results of that conversation can be documented in the fifth column. This can be a yes/no designation, red/green/yellow, or whatever is deemed appropriate. Transparency as well as open and honest dialogue are paramount.

MANAGEMENT SYSTEM AND LEADERSHIP— HOW TO DO IT

Management System and Leadership

*T*he change team proposed a management system change relating to the **roles and responsibilities** of all leaders in the organization. The key aspect of UP's system change was the launch of leader standard work, which is a management system that helps companies increase participative leadership and accountability. Leader standard work could support the Change Initiative because it focused on removing the roadblocks in implementing UP Way and ensured that key activities moved forward.

> **Management System Proposal:** Transition to leader standard work for all leaders, beginning with the CEO and cascading to all levels of the organization.

> **UP's leader standard work (LSW) definition:** Leaders approach their role with a form of work that includes mentoring and accountability.

Leader standard work is an element of UP Way that would eventually be introduced to every person who had direct reports in the Operating Department. Initially, the concept was presented to the top leadership only.

Our change team also proposed a list of leadership behaviors to the COO that aligned with UP Way and would help to introduce LSW. The proposed behaviors were:

- UP Way messaging delivered by leaders,
- UP Way training delivered by leaders,
- LSW initiated by leaders,
- Feedback results from the UP Way training survey acted upon by leaders if necessary.

The change team identified the top leaders of the Operating Department for the first round of interviews (see organizational chart). We followed this round with the leaders of the three learning trial locations.

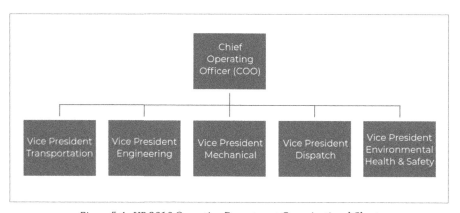

Figure 5.4: UP 2010 Operating Department Organizational Chart

We assigned individual members of the change team to describe the LSW management system to each top leader in the Operating Department and ask:

1. Do you have any concerns with the UP Way? If so, what are your major concerns?
2. Do you have any concerns about the proposed leadership behaviors and LSW (the management system)?
3. How can we best address your concerns so we can have your full support for UP Way?

The following is an excerpt from that process and involves Stephanie, the leader of the engineering team, and Grayson, engineering's representative on the change team. Engineering is responsible for the infrastructure within the railroad, such as planning and installing new infrastructure (i.e., tracks, bridges, crossing gates) and maintenance of that infrastructure.

When Grayson interviewed Stephanie about any concerns she had with UP Way, Stephanie discussed a new program called process engineering that had recently been introduced within engineering. This new program changed the way that many tasks were performed, and Stephanie was concerned that the UP Way would be confusing to people who had recently been trained in process engineering.

Grayson and Stephanie worked together to develop a strategy to alleviate Stephanie's concerns. The strategy involved mapping the items that process engineering and UP Way had in common, using process engineering terminology for those items, and introducing the elements in UP Way that process engineering did not have. This approach helped employees understand how UP Way and process engineering complimented each other. Stephanie and Grayson also agreed to a modified implementation timeframe so that employees in engineering were not inundated with new programs and new training. By taking the time to understand Stephanie's concerns and address them, the change team gained Stephanie's commitment to UP Way.

UP Way Catchball Example

Complete this at change team meeting		Complete this during meeting with leader	Complete this at next change team meeting	Complete this during discussion owner's next meeting with leader	
Leader	**Discussion Owner**	**Leader's Concerns**	**Strategy to Address Concerns**	**Results**	**Agree?**
Stephanie, Engineering Leader	Grayson	Just rolled out Process Engineering (PE). Doesn't want to confuse employees	Develop integration of UP Way & PE. Modify roll-out timeline	Stephanie happy with solution. Engineering leaders will teach and deploy leader standard work classes 2 levels down.	Yes

Figure 5.5: UP Way Catchball Example

In addition to the modified implementation schedule and the mapping to help integrate process engineering and UP Way, Stephanie agreed that LSW would help her department in multiple ways, including ensuring the sustainment of UP Way and process engineering. We will further explain LSW in the next section.

All operations leaders were approached in the same manner and their feedback was documented.

Leader Standard Work Results

UP used LSW to engage leadership in regularly scheduled one-on-one meetings with their direct reports. Leaders used these meetings to mentor and coach their employees. The meetings were also used to track the status of various projects, reinforce any ongoing initiatives, provide accountability for deliverables, and detect potential failures.

Each leader in the Operating Department was eventually trained in LSW. We defined "leader" as any person at UP who had employees who reported to him or her (direct reports). We started LSW training with the top leaders in the Operating Department then cascaded until every leader had been trained and had implemented leader standard work with his/her direct reports. The cascading activity included:

- *Leaders trained their direct reports on how to use LSW.*
- *Leaders set up individual, regular meetings with their direct reports on a cadence that worked for them.*
- *Leaders and their direct reports used an agreed-upon form that tracked activities, including UP Way progress.*
- *The completed form was reviewed at the regularly scheduled meetings where the leader helped to remove roadblocks, mentored, coached, and detected potential failures with UP Way activities.*

The following graph shows the progress check survey results regarding the effectiveness of LSW at UP.

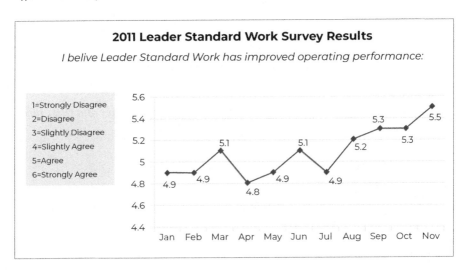

Figure 5.6: 2011 Leader Standard Work Survey Results

By November 2011, approximately 1.5 years after first introducing LSW, leaders responded that they agreed it had improved operating performance for the company. The November score of 5.5 was halfway between "agree" and "strongly agree" which was an improvement over the 4.9 "agree" score in January of that year. It was evident that LSW was taking hold and was delivering positive results; however, we continued to measure its progress check for several more years.

Practical Application: Management System and Leadership

After a few years into UP Way activities, we began to see synergies between UP Way and safety. Initially, the safety program was organized at the corporate level and each major department had its own safety coordinator. Krista led one of the large departments and was interested in exploring how her department could improve its management system and leadership behavior associated with safety activities.

In the early 2000s, the existing safety program was owned and managed by the leaders of each department rather than employee-owned. The program was rules-based, meaning that there was a list of safety rules, and managers would hand out safety violations to employees who broke the rules. The corporate safety department began promoting behavioral-based safety that could be co-owned by employees and leadership. As in any large-scale corporate change, it was difficult to get traction across the company. After learning about UP Way and seeing the employee engagement that UP Way fostered, Krista wanted to transition the rules-based management system enforced by leadership to a behavioral one shared between the leaders and the employees doing the work within her department.

Krista and her leadership team worked with the safety department to determine the best way to communicate the safety behaviors they wanted the employees to embrace. They discussed these behaviors with field employees in Krista's department and shared many practical examples. For instance, one behavior reminded employees to look both ways when crossing a train track to stay out of the path of the train. They also reminded employees about the "three points of contact" when ascending or descending. This referred to always having three points of contact when going up or down a ladder such as those found on locomotives (i.e., two hands and one foot, or one hand and two feet).

In the new system, the leadership behaviors also had to change to support this new management system. Rather than managers giving out safety violations for every unsafe activity they saw, management violations were limited to critical safety situations and leaders were encouraged to coach employees on less severe unsafe behaviors.

Initially, employees were also asked to coach each other when they saw unsafe behaviors, but they felt uncomfortable doing that. Krista realized that it was too big of a change in the management system to immediately expect employees to verbally coach each other. Instead, employees were then asked to use a safety observation card if they saw their coworkers doing any unsafe behaviors. Employees placed the completed safety observation cards anonymously in a locked box which was opened by the union leader once a week. The safety coordinator then made a graph of the number of times each incident was mentioned to determine the areas with the biggest opportunity for improvement. These focus areas were displayed and discussed each month with all field employees in Krista's department. Employees were also asked to think of improvements.

Gradually, the trust was established so that the employees no longer needed to file anonymous cards but instead could talk to each other about safety. Once that occurred, the rule-based safety management system transformed into a shared, behavior-based system that was strongly supported by both the leaders and employees doing the work.

Was all of it worth it? Absolutely. After the third year of the change, Krista's department reduced its injury rate by 50 percent and received recognition for the best safety record of the department's peers within the industry. Several *years after that, the department reduced its injury rate in half again, and continued ongoing improvements.*

Everyone's favorite villain when it comes to botched change efforts is "leadership." Leadership may fail to become engaged, which is one kind of problem, or perhaps even more difficult, they may be engaged but their behaviors were born of decades of leading successfully via methods or styles that no longer match the needs of the new situation. Meanwhile, "management" or "the management system" gets short shrift in the form of no treatment at all or is dismissed as something to simply do away with as strategy guru Gary Hamel advocated in *the Harvard Business Review* article "First, Let's Fire All the Managers."

But, what if, instead of mere overseers to enforce compliance, managers at every level are *supporters*, offering coaching and mentoring to aid in the learning of new skills and encouragement to keep spirits and motivation high? If we decide to aim for that as a vision, the challenge becomes how to devise a management *system* that both requires and reinforces intentionally designed to achieve it.

The management system, then, represents the various dials that leaders have at their disposal to direct (to *manage*) the organization, both their own slice of it, but also the communication channels, meeting structures, decision forums, formal gatherings, strategic planning and budgeting processes, daily management routines, and other conduits that constitute connections and inform the nature of actions throughout the organization.

Thus, as Lynn shares in her description of the situation at UP, practices you may employ such as leader standard work, teamwork within and between organizational silos, and communication for shared understanding, will be enabled by behaviors that represent our best selves in action at work. In fact, combining these two independent matters (the management system and leader behaviors) into one Change Question may not seem intuitive, and you may choose to address them separately, but combining them is one way to emphasize the deep relationship between the two. Leadership behaviors and management systems are intertwined. Still, when it comes time to address the two, you will need to consider each in its own right as well as together.

Note that the perspective of this chapter is from that of a change agent and/or change team, tagged with the assignment of bringing about specific change. However, in many if not most circumstances, the change is led directly by a member of the executive team (in fact, even if there is a formal change team, the team will require executive sponsorship). The executive may be tasked with changing his or her peers and with (deep breath here) changing oneself at the same time. A challenging task.

Especially during times of leading major change, you'll need to negotiate (as I imagine Lynn did at UP) the balance between push and pull. You may need to exercise some push to overcome inertia (a.k.a. resistance to change) yet you want to encourage everyone in the organization to pull for your support as they grasp the new direction and learn the new skills they need. How to provide just enough direction so that people know which way to go, yet not so much instruction that you take away the ownership you need them to take? It's a space that is neither command and control nor laissez-faire. As Alfred North Whitehead stated, "The art of progress is to preserve order amid change and to preserve change amid order."

You may find that leader behaviors in your organization are where they need to be and well-suited for the specific change you are instituting. Or your situation may require or provide an opportunity to reconsider the ways leadership is exercised in your organization. In such a case, you can choose among various leadership models, such as Robert Greenleaf's well-known Servant Leadership; the late Edgar Schein's model of Humble Leadership; or Jeff Liker's and Gary Convis's four-point model for Lean Leadership: (1) commit to self-development, (2) coach and develop others, (3) daily management and kaizen, (4) create a vision and align goals. Or, even better, you may choose aspects of any of these or others to create your own blended model. Whatever you choose, you will also want to build a management system that reinforces it even as it directs your organization toward its performance aspirations at the same time.

Whatever specific leadership model and management system you may adopt, a dimension that will be critical to include is what Amy Edmondson, who we also reference in chapter 4, calls "psychological safety." As she explained in *The Fearless Organization: Creating Psychological Safety in the Workplace for Learning, Innovation, and Growth*—informed by compelling research of practices in the safest healthcare organizations—a psychologically safe workplace environment is one where each individual feels enabled to openly share his or her thinking and feeling. In studying healthcare team performance, Edmondson found, to her initial surprise, that higher-performing teams (teams with better outcomes) reported more problems than did less successful teams. Analysis showed that it was the level of mutual trust and psychological safety that enabled members to question, call out problems, and offer ideas that led to improved performance. Squeakier wheels can lead to better performance and psychological safety enables wheels to squeak when they need to. If we want those who know the work best—those who *do* the work—to commit to actively pursue our aspirational organization, leaders can lead the way by creating a psychologically safe environment.

Summary

This section is meant to remind you of the importance of a management system that reinforces the Change Initiative and visible, behavioral leadership commitment over and above lip service. In the UP example, the management system of leader standard work may seem like more than your organization needs. Your organization and your change team may choose completely different (and simpler) methods than UP to gain visible leadership support for your Change Initiative.

YOUR TURN

Refer to the guide at the end of this book when you are ready to work through the management system and leadership element of the Change Questions. The digital workbook contains many of the forms shown in this chapter in a fillable PDF format.

06

Understand Your Culture

Figure 6.1: Change Questions Diagram - Culture

*W*hen I was being interviewed for the position at UP, I asked my favorite question, "Tell me about the culture here." I was surprised at the consistency in the answers I received from the people who were interviewing me. People said things like, "I am proud to work at UP." "UP is like a family." "We work as a team." "We have strong traditions." "People come here and

Lynn's STORY

never leave." During my first week at the company, I was amazed at how many people said, "You will love working here." Another thing I found interesting was when I was introduced at various meetings, people went around the room and told me their names, titles, and how long they had been at the company. I expected to hear names and titles, but not years of service. I understood then that people really don't leave UP. It wasn't unusual to have at least half the people around the table with twenty-plus years of service at UP.

I was beginning to understand the culture at UP but was only seeing the tip of the iceberg. I needed to understand the strengths and weaknesses of UP's culture and what made it unique. The answers to the culture Change Question still felt amorphous to me, and I wanted to know if UP had a culture that was open to change.

N otice that culture is placed firmly in the center of the Change Questions diagram and extends toward all of the other activities. This visually represents the way that culture permeates all areas of the Change Questions methodology. This chapter is meant for reflection, both for the change leader and members of the change team.

You may wonder why we placed culture as the final chapter (before developing the iterative implementation plan), rather than have it come earlier in the process. We have done so because throughout the process of your change team moving through the Change Questions, we have created touch points with culture. When you considered context in design, do, and improve the work, you were considering culture. When you set up learning trials and involved the employees in feedback loops, culture was front and center. When you gathered FAQs, this helped give you direct access to cultural considerations of the employee base. And when you reviewed your existing management system, you were, in large part, assessing culture. It is critical and needs to be considered here and is also addressed in every step taken to this point.

What is Culture?

The foundation of any organization rests on the fundamental *thinking* or culture of that organization. Take a moment to consider Edgar Schein's iconic definition of organizational culture:

> **"The culture of a group can now be defined as a pattern of shared basic assumptions that was learned by a group as it solved its problems of external adaptation and internal integration, that has worked well enough to be considered valid and, therefore, to be taught to new members as the correct way to perceive, think, and feel in relation to those problems."**
>
> — EDGAR SCHEIN, *ORGANIZATIONAL CULTURE AND LEADERSHIP: A DYNAMIC VIEW.*

If you believe that Schein's definition of culture is accurate, it is evident that the often elusive but pervasive culture of your organization will play a big role in the success—or lack thereof—of your Change Initiative. Unfortunately, many initiators of change ignore culture and its impact on the change. They develop excellent strategies for change paired with detailed implementation plans in a vacuum as if the organization's culture is non-existent.

Change Question

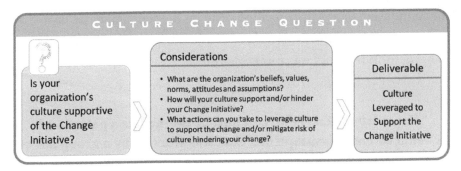

Figure 6.2: Culture Change Question

The Impact of Culture on Your Change Initiative

Once you answer the Change Question and articulate the culture of your organization, take a step back and think about the change that you will be implementing. Reflect on how the organization's culture may impact it. In other words, how will the culture support the initiative and contribute to its success? By leveraging the aspects of culture that will support your initiative, you can access a powerful tool to aid in its adoption. On the flip side, how might the culture of your organization hinder the success of your initiative? Your answer will help you to determine how you can mitigate the risk of failure.

Here are several examples of how to think about this:

If your culture is top-down and autocratic:

- Support: The initiative may be implemented very quickly because the leaders simply have to tell everyone to do things the new way, and the changes will be done.

- Hinder: Although the initiative may appear to be implemented quickly, its long-term sustainment may be hampered because people may not truly buy into it, as many people don't like to be told what to do, even though they initially go through the motions of participating in it.

If your culture is creative and innovative:

- Support: People will be open to change and gladly embrace it. They may also improve the change through innovation.

- Hinder: Because the organization is used to things constantly changing, the initiative may be perceived as "flavor of the month" and may not be taken seriously.

Once you've determined the impact of culture on your initiative, you can decide if you need to take any additional actions. Look at the ways your culture will support it. Ask yourself and your change team if you can leverage that support any further.

Conversely, if your culture seems like it will work against your initiative, think about how you can mitigate that risk. Again, you may already have done so in previous steps. If not, you can determine mitigation actions at this time.

Culture

*O*nce the team was formed and had completed most of the questions, we discussed our impressions of UP's culture. We defined UP's culture as follows:

UP's culture is long-standing with strong traditions and seasoned employees. People are proud to work at UP. There is a focus on relationships and teamwork. Employees work hard, get the job done, and overcome difficult situations. There is a dedication to customer service. The company tends to be siloed according to departmental structure and risk averse.

In looking at how the culture could support and hinder the initiative; this is what we surmised:

- *Support: The pride in the company would help people feel pride in the accomplishments that they would achieve through the UP Way. The team focus would fit well with the team projects utilized in the UP Way. Once UP Way was established, the strong traditions and the longevity of the workforce would help the UP Way sustain and become a part of the way the company operates.*

- *Hinder: Employees' pride in the company might make them unwilling to imitate other companies that have implemented programs that are similar to the UP Way. The family-like atmosphere might make it difficult for people to express their true feelings if they don't think the UP Way would be good for the company; they may go through the motions but not really support change. The risk-averse culture and longevity of the workforce might make them resistant to changing the way they currently do things. The siloed structure may prohibit cross-functional success.*

In channeling the culture to support the UP Way, we saw that the actions we had planned throughout the Change Questions would indeed adequately support it. For example, strong communication alongside our recognition plans would leverage the pride aspect of our culture. We also saw that the design of the work would be supported by the teamwork aspect of the culture. We could use progress checks to quickly detect if UP Way was not being sustained so that we could catch early failure and turn it around. We hoped that eventually UP Way would just be part of UP's tradition.

We felt that most of the risks of the culture hindering the UP Way had been mitigated within the Change Questions. For example, in the "hinder" paragraph, we noted that some leaders may go through the motions, but not really support UP Way. Both the panel survey and the training surveys would detect if leaders were going through the motions. The one risk we had not adequately mitigated was the siloed nature of UP's departmental structure. So, we specifically added a plan to tackle some long-term, difficult problems that had not been solved previously because they were cross-departmental. We knew that if we could get cross-departmental successes, we could recognize them and begin to break down the departmental silos.

Practical Application: Culture

A mantra within UP was: "So goes velocity, so goes customer satisfaction."

Carlos was tasked with improving velocity on a corridor within his region. The problem Carlos had was that his slow corridor (and all corridors in general) involved a multitude of departments that handled a multitude of tasks to keep the trains running efficiently—and not all of the departments reported to Carlos. Culturally, each department tended to work in its own space, optimizing its own processes, which may or may not give preference to the region's highest priority corridors. Since Carlos's corridor improvement task came from Tarek, a leader in the Operating Department, Carlos knew he had the support from operating leadership to begin to work cross-functionally on his slow corridor.

Carlos scheduled a three-day rail trip on a train that included sleeping cars, a conference room, and an observation car. The glass-enclosed observation car was the very last car on the train with tiered theater-type seats all facing the track at the rear of the train. Carlos invited forty people to join him on the train. The invitees represented centralized and decentralized departments with union and non-union employees. These employees came from departments such as track maintenance, signal, dispatch, telecom, and mechanical.

As the train crawled along at a maximum speed of 30 mph, it made frequent stops so that the experts on the train could examine the corridor at close range and brainstorm opportunities to improve velocity. At the end of the three days, Carlos had a list of items that once implemented would improve velocity. He also had a commitment from each of the departments to give these items a high priority.

It took four years to complete all of the items, but within two years the corridor had gone from being one of the slowest corridors in the region to one of the top five in terms of velocity. These improvements boosted the service unit's metrics, and together, helped UP achieve record velocity. Since each delayed train causes problems downstream, the benefits extended well beyond the service unit itself.

The common assertion often attributed to Peter Drucker that "culture eats strategy for breakfast" may be the most well-known of axioms stressing the importance of corporate culture to any change or any major Change Initiative of a company. It's hard to disagree. If true, accounting for culture must lie at the heart of any major initiative.

While I am among those who agree with assertions such as Professor Drucker's, I have also long advised caution about attempting to change culture directly or certainly avoiding doing so at the beginning of an improvement initiative. Rather, first focus on clarifying the problems you need to solve, work on how you can solve them, and build, with *intention*, effective human relationships along the way. This will steer you toward your preferred culture, which you can continuously nurture, with *intention*, as you go about pursuing the organization's mission. Even Edgar Schein, who Lynn quotes above and who gave us the very term organizational culture, cautions that it is a fool's mission to try to directly change the culture itself—rather, focus on building collaborative relationships in service of the mission at hand.

Note also that in Lynn's story of leading change at UP, the importance of creating connections and collaborative relationships between organizational silos (functions, departments, etc.) cannot be overstated. There are the mechanical pieces of a change process, but it's the more organic, softer dimensions that will make it work to achieve deep change. Jim Benson's book *The Collaboration Equation* is a great resource to help you with the principles and some processes of creating a collaborative culture.

As Benson states, silos or silo-thinking can "slow productive conversations, stifle decisionmaking, crush growth, and create rampant zero-sum games. But we can break that vicious cycle of engineering versus marketing versus HR versus etc. We can build low-overhead systems of collaboration that run on good decisions made by informed professionals at the right time."

In the end, you will indeed desire a culture that represents what you wish the organization to be. Jamie Bonini, president of Toyota's own Toyota Production System Support Center describes the Toyota Production System—which is often misunderstood as a simple technical work improvement system—as "an organizational culture of highly engaged people solving problems and innovating to drive performance that is created and sustained by a three-part system of philosophy, technical elements, and managerial role to engage and develop people."At the end of the day, culture change accompanies any major Change Initiative.

Understand your culture, try the methods Lynn describes in her Change Initiative at UP or others that you may find to envision and even design the culture you deem appropriate for your organization and its aspirations. From there you can begin practicing your way to new ways of thinking and a new culture as you undertake to achieve your desired change through (next chapter) *iterative implementation*.

Summary

The culture of your organization will touch all elements of your Change Initiative. Your team's beliefs, values, norms, attitudes, and assumptions will be key in driving the behaviors of the people within your Change Initiative. It is essential that you and your change team have a good grasp of the impact that culture will play on your initiative, including how it may support or hinder the change.

YOUR TURN

Refer to the guide at the end of this book when you are ready to work through the culture element of the Change Questions. The digital workbook contains several forms in a fillable PDF format.

Create Your Iterative
Implementation Plan

Figure 7.1: Change Questions Diagram

"A goal without a plan is just a wish."

— Antoine de Saint-Exupery, *The Little Prince*

ITERATIVE IMPLEMENTATION—WHAT TO DO

*O*ur change team had been getting pressure throughout the planning process to "just go implement UP Way already!" Many leaders weren't used to doing prep work before a Change Initiative. We were all excited to be at the point where we could begin introducing UP Way to the masses through our implementation plan. But wait … I had to break the news to the change team and leadership that our implementation plan would have the word "iterative" in front of it. That meant it wasn't a go-go-go plan, but a go-evaluate-go plan. This would take a little longer, but deliver oh, so much better results.

Finally! We are at the last formal step—the part that you are probably MOST familiar with, the implementation plan! Sadly, many times when change is being implemented, the only step in the planning phase of the Change Initiative is the implementation plan. Notice that we have added the word, "iterative" because we believe that it is detrimental to the initiative to blindly follow a pre-determined implementation plan without including feedback loops to ensure that the change is truly adding value.

Your organization may also have its own terminology for an implementation plan. Some organizations call it a "deployment plan" or a "project plan." It is simply a step-by-step process that is used to implement a Change Initiative. Framing is important, but don't get too hung up on nomenclature. Choose what works well for you and your organization.

Implementation Question

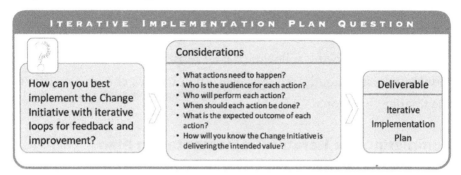

Figure 7.2: Iterative Implementation Plan Question

Iterative Implementation Plan Overview

Many organizations work long and hard to create a nuts-and-bolts plan for implementation. They assume that they can release the plan and go on autopilot while the implementation takes place. The primary metric for success is adherence to the plan and the plan's deadlines.

Unfortunately, there is no such thing as a perfect implementation plan or a perfect Change Initiative. You may find that certain aspects of your plan aren't working well and need to be adjusted or outright removed. Timelines work well as guidelines, but if the team marches forward to a set timeline without correcting small failures along the way, the team may have the great accomplishment of completing the plan on time but delivering substandard results.

We urge you to think about your implementation plan as a living, iterative document that is open to revision and opportunities for learning in service of continuously improving the overall initiative. The primary measure of success for the implementation of your Change Initiative should NOT be that the plan is completed on time. It should be that the change is successfully implemented, delivers the expected results, and *sustains*. On-time completion of the deliverables is important, but it's not the MOST important thing.

In general, it helps if your iterative implementation plan includes the elements shown in the following table. Most of these items are commonly understood and used; however, the progress check is specific to the Change Questions.

Completing the Iterative Implementation Plan

Iterative Implementation Plan Template

Action	Audience	Ownership	Target Date	Proposed Outcome	Progress Check (if applicable)

Figure 7.3: Iterative Implementation Plan Form

We have included this form in the digital workbook. If you have a preferred project planning system within your organization, feel free to use that method, and add the items that are often missing in traditional project planning tools such as the progress checks. Remember, the progress checks ensure the *iterative improvement* of the plan and the Change Initiative. The following steps will help you complete your iterative implementation plan.

1 **Action:** Determine what actions are necessary to launch the change. If the change is straightforward, you can usually write the actions sequentially in the first column of the iterative implementation plan with

very little effort. If you have a complex change, you may want to start with a brainstorming approach and sequence the actions after you've listed them.

After you have listed all the action items you can think of, review your answers to the Change Questions to ensure that the implementation actions generated from the Change Questions are also identified within the iterative implementation plan. For example, in the recognition section, you may have created an approach to gather success stories for publication. You will want to include actions around recognition in the iterative implementation plan. The following list identifies items that are frequently added to the iterative implementation plan. Keep in mind that every Change Initiative is different, so only use the items that apply to your implementation, and in the order that suits it best.

Potential Actions from the Change Questions to Include in the Iterative Implementation Plan:

- Initiate communication plan elements such as a vision statement and key messages.
- Distribute FAQs.
- Enable capability with tools and resources.
- Begin training and development.
- Launch learning trials.
- Implement management system changes.
- Reinforce leadership behaviors.
- Provide recognition for success.
- Analyze progress check data.
- Act upon progress check data to improve the initiative.
- Incorporate any additional actions relating to culture.

2 **Audience:** Record who will be the recipient of the action.

3 Ownership: Determine who is responsible for leading or performing the action (person/team/department).

4 Target Date: Enter the proposed completion date of the action. Sort the document by target date.

5 Proposed Outcome: There is a relationship between the action column of what needs to happen and the proposed outcome column of the anticipated deliverable. In other words—how you know it's done. The proposed outcome is generally written as a metric goal, and it will reflect the proof that you have accomplished "what will be done." You will see several examples of this when we return to the UP story at the end of this chapter.

6 Progress Check: The progress check is a new or existing measurement activity that provides feedback on the amount of expected value to be derived from the Change Initiative.

As a reminder, we discussed progress checks in chapter 3. Progress checks flowed from the value statements we introduced in chapter 2. During this step in framework, you will populate the progress check column in the iterative implementation plan with progress check measures that correspond with any value statements that may be referenced in the action column.

Not all items in your iterative implementation plan will have a progress check; however, all your progress checks will have an action. Remember that the purpose of the progress check is to measure if the expected value is being obtained by the change. Your implementation plan will contain many essential tasks that do not need a progress check but will still have a target date column to ensure that the action has been completed. Every progress check that you identified in the improve the work section should be listed on your plan.

To illustrate this further, let's expand on the billing system example presented in chapter 3.

Billing Example - Value Statement and Progress Check

Value Statement	Progress Check
The new billing system will reduce the number of billing errors.	Number of billing errors (pre-training vs. post-training)

Figure 7.4: Billing Example Value Statement and Progress Check

A high-level iterative implementation plan for the new billing system might look like this:

Example: High Level Iterative Implementation Plan for Billing System

Action	Audience	Ownership	Target Date	Proposed Outcome	Progress Check (if applicable)
Hold department meeting to announce new billing system	All billing dept. employees	Billing dept. manager	June 1	100% of billing dept. employees know about new billing system	n/a
Train billing department employees in new system	All billing dept. employees	Billing dept. manager	June 15	100% of billing dept. employees trained in new billing system	n/a
Utilize new billing system	All billing dept. employees	Billing dept. manager	June 30	100% of billing dept. empls are using new system	Number of billing errors (pre vs. post)

Figure 7.5: Example of High-Level Iterative Implementation Plan for Billing System

Notice that the first two steps (rows) do not relate directly to the value statement and therefore do not need a progress check—but will be checked for completion by the indicated target date. However, the third step—utilize the new billing system—has a progress check associated with it that involves improvement in billing errors.

The progress checks continually provide feedback on the effectiveness of the initiative in delivering value. As a recap, when you developed the value statements, we recommended you use the first two S.M.A.R.T. goals of specific and measurable.

- Specific: Target a specific area for improvement.
- Measurable: Quantify or suggest an indicator of progress.
- Assignable: Specify who will do it.
- Realistic: State what results can realistically be achieved, given available resources.
- Time-related: Specify when the result(s) can be achieved.

You then developed the progress checks from the value statements.

Examples of Value Statements and Corresponding Progress Checks

Value Statement	Progress Check
The new billing system will reduce the number of billing errors	Number of billing errors (pre-training minus post-training)
Value Statement	**Progress Check**
The new organizational chart will streamline customer interactions	■ Customer satisfaction survey results ■ Number of customer "touch points" ■ Time involved to resolve customer issues
Value Statement	**Progress Check**
The new process for switching railcars will reduce yard dwell time	■ Dwell time metrics (pre-post)

Figure 7.6: Examples of Value Statements and Corresponding Progress Checks

Now, in this step of the process, when you place the progress checks into the iterative implementation plan, the corresponding columns allow completion of the S.M.A.R.T. objective because they identify that progress checks will be Assignable (ownership), Realistic (proposed outcome), and Time-related (target date).

Iterative Implementation Plan

G*iven the complexity of deploying the UP Way to 42,000 employees in different locations, departments, and roles, our implementation plan had many steps and needed to be iterative. We developed an initial iterative implementation plan for the three learning trials. As the change team gathered feedback on the effectiveness of the activities within the learning trials, we regularly revised and improved the iterative implementation plan for use in the next UP Way launch, beyond the learning trials, and eventually for all the operating departments.*

As a reminder, the change team identified five value statements for the UP Way that had corresponding progress checks.

UP Way Value Statements and Progress Checks

Value Statement	Progress Check
Empowered employees improve customer service	■ Panel Survey ■ Customer Service Metrics
UP Way improves safety and operational performance	■ Pre-Post Training Surveys ■ Panel Survey ■ Operational Results ■ Safety Performance Results
Employees are skilled in UP Way concepts and are using them in the workplace.	■ Pre-Post Training Surveys ■ Panel Survey
We are building a problem-solving culture.	■ Number of active UP Way projects led by employees ■ Results metrics of UP Way projects ■ Sustainment metrics of UP Way projects
UP Way builds employee engagement	■ Pre-Post Training Surveys ■ Annual Engagement Survey Scores ■ Panel Survey

Figure 7.7: UP Way Value Statements and Progress Checks

The next chart shows a portion of the UP Way change team's iterative implementation plan.

UP Way Iterative Implementation Plan

Action	Audience	Ownership	Target Date	Proposed Outcome	Progress Check (If applicable)
Kick-off learning trials with UP Way Overview Training	Service Unit leadership in learning trial locations	Sr. operating leadership with CI support	Oct 30	100% learning trial Service Unit leadership trained in UP Way overview	■ Pre-Post Training Surveys
Train leadership in leader standard work (LSW) and begin to implement LSW	Service Unit leadership in learning trial locations	Super-intendent of Service Unit with CI support	Nov 30	100% learning trial Service Unit leadership trained in LSW	■ Pre-Post Training Surveys ■ Panel Survey
Hold informational & feedback meeting with union leadership in learning trial locations	Union leadership in learning trial locations	Super-intendent	Nov 30	Gathered union feedback	n/a
Set-up Help Line and mentors for learning trial locations	Employees in learning trial locations	CI leadership	Nov 30	Functioning Help Line	n/a

Figure 7.8: UP Way Iterative Implementation Plan

The actions in the first two rows involve training. Since the change team developed pre-post surveys for all training as progress checks, we could gather data on some of the value statements whenever we did training. The training surveys covered more than just training. There were also questions asking if the UP Way was adding value in areas such as employee engagement and operating performance. In addition, the panel survey, another progress check, specifically asked questions regarding UP Way elements of standard work and LSW. Since the action in the second row referenced LSW, we knew that we could gather progress check information from the panel survey relating to it.

The action in the third row related to a meeting with the union leadership at each of the learning trial locations. We had included union leadership at the national level in some of our preliminary discussions regarding the UP Way; however, once we chose the learning trial locations, it was critical to involve the local union leadership in discussions about how we envisioned UP Way operating within their locations and to gather feedback from them on how we could improve UP Way activity as it related to their members. Notice, that the proposed outcome associated with the third row identified the gathering of union feedback but did not have a progress check that was applicable at that early stage. In a later step in the iterative implementation plan, union members began to get trained. The training activity was associated with a progress check (pre-post training surveys), as well as the panel survey progress check since the majority of people in the panel survey were union members.

The action in the fourth row was identified when the change team reviewed the resources needed within the capability building section of the Change Questions process (see chapter 4: Engage and Develop Employees). When we worked through the capability building section, we felt it was necessary to provide the resources of a helpline and mentorship. We then reflected on that action in the iterative implementation plan with an implementation target date.

As we moved through implementation of the iterative implementation plan during the UP Way launch, we used the methods in the next chapter to ensure that the Change Initiative was going as planned and to make necessary improvements as we went along.

It is healthy to presume that everything can be improved all of the time because, firstly, we humans are always learning, and, secondly, conditions are always changing anyway, demanding adjustment. There is no perfect plan. Still, to be able to continuously

improve through PDCA (see chapter 3), you need to start with something - you need the first P. You can't do PDCA without the "P." We need plans ... even knowing that they will likely change.

But what is a plan? What is its purpose? We often think of a plan as *something to adhere to*. A blueprint to follow exactly. Yet, a two-fold truism I learned to consider early in my career is that (1) plans always change, and (2) things don't go according to plan anyway. Therefore, plan accordingly. In other words, plan on things not going according to plan!

Build into your plan contingencies and, most importantly as Lynn illustrates in her story, build in means by which you can know how the plan is proceeding and where adjustments may become necessary. As author of the *High-Velocity Edge,* Steve Spear wisely describes a plan as "an experiment you run to see what you don't understand ... ." Far indeed from the traditional notion of a plan.

In their book *Designing the Future*, Jim Morgan and Jeff Liker describe a dynamic process for managing to a plan which includes a detailed process and cadence for *reviews as learning sessions*, a time and process to check and see where the organization may be struggling and to decide on countermeasures that may be helpful to provide support. PDCA in this way may occur in very quick cycles or in cycles of months or years. Different situations call for different cadences. As Morgan recounts from his experience with the weekly business plan review (BPR) that CEO Alan Mulally instituted upon his arrival at Ford in 2006, "The BPR created a natural PDCA cadence and framework for the leadership team ... This practice then flowed throughout the entire organization ... By constantly learning together and adjusting as required, they were able to steer the organization through some of the most turbulent times in modern business history."

To say that plans change and we adjust dynamically does not mean that we don't plan, or that we don't plan in great detail! The more detail we include, the better experiments we can run, knowing more precisely whether things are unfolding as expected. Hence the value in the examples and tools such as those that Lynn shares in this chapter. Give them a try. Just don't be surprised when things don't unfold as your carefully laid plans indicated! This leads us to the critical next chapter about dynamically managing and improving your change process itself.

Summary

This chapter covered the development of your iterative implementation plan. In the next chapter, we'll discuss how you will use it. All the preparation that you have done throughout the Change Questions methodology has led to this plan. You have increased the probability that your Change Initiative will succeed and with iterative implementation, you will continue to learn and improve your initiative based on the feedback you invite and receive as you go.

YOUR TURN

Refer to the guide at the end of this book when you are ready to work through the iterative implementation plan. The digital workbook contains the forms shown in this chapter which are in a fillable PDF format.

Support and Improve
Your Change Initiative

Figure 8.1: Change Questions Diagram

*B*y the time the UP change team got to the implementation step, you'd think we would have been exhausted. But working through this last step, actually implementing the plan, was my favorite part of the whole process. Instead of our implementation plan being a dead, dry thing at UP, we made it feel alive and fun. Really! Don't believe me? Judge for yourself—

Two primary areas are important in this launch phase:

1. Supporting the iterative implementation plan through managing, tracking, and ownership, and

2. Listening, learning, and improving the implementation of the Change Initiative.

Implementation Questions

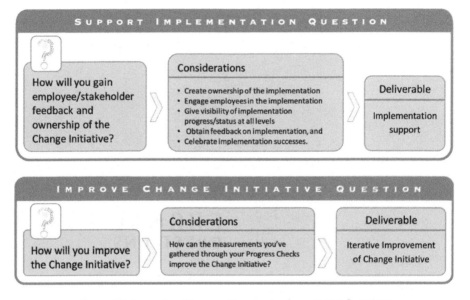

Figure 8.2: Support and Improve Iterative Implementation Questions

SUPPORT IMPLEMENTATION—WHAT TO DO

Managing, Tracking, and Owning the Change

Just because you developed an implementation plan, it does not mean that people will respect it or follow it! It is advisable to actively support the work you are proposing through managing, tracking, and creating ownership around the plan. There are various ways to do this. Some of you may already have project management software that includes tools such as a timeline, critical path, or a matrix format to track project implementation. Most of you are probably familiar with the red, yellow, and green charts that are often used to track projects. If you decide to use the iterative implementation plan format within this book, an easy way to produce this type of tracking system is to add a column to your plan, as shown here and in the digital workbook.

Iterative Implementation Plan with Tracking Column Added

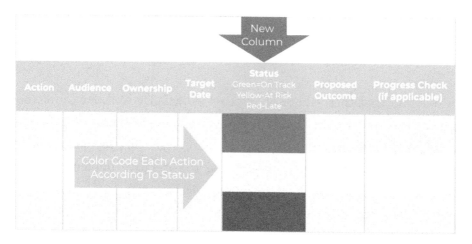

Figure 8.3: Iterative Implementation Plan with Tracking Column Added

When items have been completed, you can remove them or keep them for a record. You may use a check mark or other identification to show that the items have been completed.

Iterative Implementation Plan with Completion

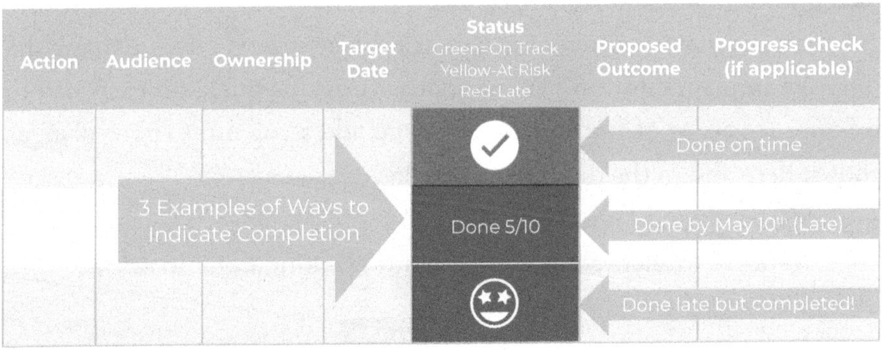

Figure 8.4: Iterative Implementation Plan with Completion

We find that these types of systems work fairly well but can be so much more effective if you display the iterative implementation plan in a prominent location, and if the change team establishes regularly scheduled updates while actively referencing the iterative implementation plan on display. This can be done in a physical location or remotely with video calls for progress updates.

We have rarely implemented a change that does *not* have these three elements:

1. Easily understandable visual indication of the status of each action of the iterative implementation plan along with target dates and ownership.

2. Displaying the iterative implementation plan in a prominent location, ideally where the change is taking place, and/or in an electronic format that allows easy access by remote team members.

3. Regularly scheduled updates by the people responsible for the implementation actions in a format where everyone involved in the change can be present remotely or in person.

Visual Control Boards and Workplace Walks

Some of you may be familiar with visual control boards, which are also known as huddle boards, workplace boards, whiteboards, or gemba boards. Visual control boards are generally located where the work takes place so that all employees can have access to the information displayed on the boards.

In this chapter, we refer to the boards as visual control boards. During a Change Initiative, we have had great success with using the boards to depict the status of the implementation plan. These boards can be on a flipchart stand, whiteboard, wall, window, computer screen, or anything that provides a prominent display location.

The visual control boards are then paired with regularly scheduled workplace walks. During these walks or visits, leadership will spend time with the employees who are doing the work. The workplace walk is generally held in front of the visual control boards. Employees then provide updates relating to the activities shown on the visual control board. The discussion of the board includes the goal of transparency, team-based analysis, and mutual understanding along with, of course, solving problems and making improvements!

So, for example, if your Change Initiative occurs on the manufacturing floor, the appropriate place for the board is on your manufacturing floor. Your change team will regularly meet in front of the board along with the employees who are implementing the change to discuss the status of the actions, successes, problems, and challenges. Each person whose name is in the ownership column of the iterative implementation plan would present the status of his/her action item. We have also successfully used online visual control boards paired with remote video calls that together serve as workplace walks.

When combined, the boards and workplace walks do the following:

- Create ownership through visual designation and report-outs,
- Engage employees in the change and iterative implementation plan by providing regular updates, gleaning feedback/improvement ideas,
- Develop employees by giving them experience in presenting their work to leadership,
- Give visibility to all levels of the organization,
- Celebrate successes,
- Remove roadblocks, and
- Track Change Initiative progress.

Frequency of the Workplace Walks

The frequency of your walks will very much depend upon the situation and the level of complexity of your Change Initiative. You can determine whether the walks should be daily, weekly, monthly, or some other cadence. Since the research described earlier in this book indicated that potential failure of Change Initiatives is usually evident during the first month, it may be necessary for leaders and participants to take more frequent walks at the beginning of the implementation with less frequent walks over time.

SUPPORTING IMPLEMENTATION—HOW TO DO IT

Supporting Implementation

During the launch of the UP Way, we relied on leader standard work and visual control boards with workplace walks to help support the iterative implementation plan. Since leader standard work was explained in chapter 5, we will dedicate this portion of the book to visual control boards and workplace

walks. *This chapter showcases numerous boards at UP which demonstrates the flexibility and versatility of the various types of boards.*

There are many ways to create engaging visual control boards. Often people will enlarge the color-coded iterative implementation plan and place a copy of it on the board. That is one way to do it, but we have found that it is not as engaging as a board that allows for personalization and interaction. That said, at UP, we encouraged the workgroups to find the method that worked best for them, the Change Initiative, and (if applicable) to accommodate remote employees. Each of the following examples has a different aspect that is reflective of the team's preferences and needs.

This magnetic board was in a hallway that was highly trafficked by all levels of employees, including leadership. The gold horizontal lines indicate the progress of the activity. The vertical black lines show the percentage of completion (25, 50, 75) from left to right. The blue indicators on the left denote the action to be completed, and the photos show each team that was responsible for completing each action. The team members gathered to discuss the status of their actions on a regularly scheduled basis. Leadership would attend these sessions. As the action moved closer to completion, a team member would physically move the magnetized team photo to the new completion status as shown in the second photo.

Figure 8.5: Visual Control Board Team Photos

Figure 8.6: Visual Control Board Movement

This next photo shows the iterative implementation plan for a new enterprise resource planning system that was in the IT Department's workroom. Team members gave daily updates at the end of each day for approximately five months. This was clearly a complex project. The entire process was laid out under the team photos across the top of the board (i.e., not started, process map, and functional specifications). The color-coded sticky notes behind each photo corresponded with the person responsible for the tasks shown in the rows below the photos. The rows designate three different iterations of the process and the tasks to be done.

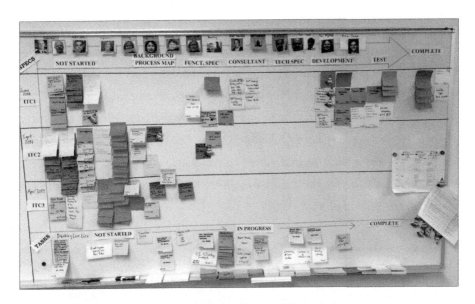

Figure 8.7: Visual Control Board - IT Department

The next board shows a process of similar complexity. You'll see that the board is actually a piece of film that adheres to a wall, as shown in the smaller photo on the right. Using presentation sheets like these allow the team to place the boards in locations that make the most sense in terms of visibility by all involved in the change.

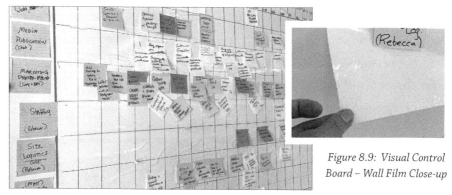

Figure 8.9: *Visual Control Board – Wall Film Close-up*

Figure 8.8: *Visual Control Board - Wall Film*

This board capitalizes on a football field theme and was developed during football season. The previous visual control board had a beach/summer theme. The shapes have different meanings in terms of process steps, and the rectangles in the column on the far left indicate who is responsible for the actions in that row. The goal was to move the action across the field until a touchdown-or, a completed action occurred. Employees gave monthly updates in front of the board and moved their projects down the field.

Figure 8.10: *Visual Control Board - Themed*

This board uses business card magnets available at most office supply stores that are sticky on one side and magnetized on the other. Color-coded tasks are stuck to the magnets, and round magnets in red, yellow, and green are used to show the status of each item. Using magnetic cards to represent tasks made for easy reprioritizing and movement.

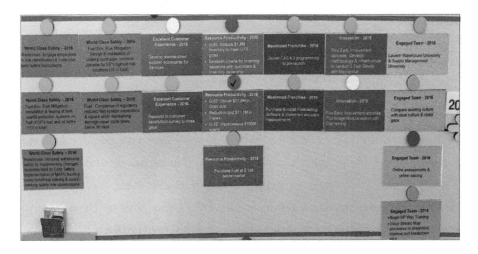

Figure 8.11: Visual Control Board - Color-Coded Magnets

This is a simple visual control board that mirrors a typical iterative implementation plan with left-to-right target dates, color-code status, actions, and ownership (not shown).

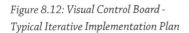

Figure 8.12: Visual Control Board - Typical Iterative Implementation Plan

This board highlights another example of a simple visual control board where the bottom right date of each rectangle indicates the target date, and the top left date in each rectangle is the day it was done. The color-coded magnet indicates if it was late (red), on time, or done (green), or slightly late/ at risk (yellow). You can see the iterative implementation plan tasks are on the top row, and correspond to process steps. Process step details were outlined in another document and the anticipated target week in the iterative implementation plan.

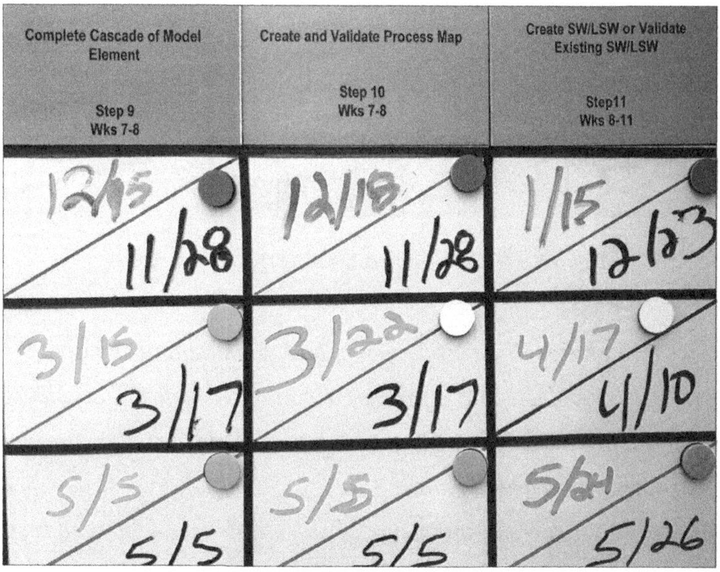

Figure 8.13: Visual Control Board - Dates and Steps

Most of the boards you have seen so far involved hand-written updates, magnets, and photos. We generally like to use these interactive elements to engage people in the board itself. As the following photo shows, it is also possible to use printouts that are updated before each workplace walk and then described during the walk.

Figure 8.14: Visual Control Board - Printed Documents

The next two photos illustrate a workplace walk held in the area where the people who were involved in the process actually worked. All employees gathered around during these regularly scheduled workplace walks. The visual control boards in this area are movable.

The first photo is a close-up of one of the employees who was responsible for updating the department regarding the status of his work noted on the visual control board. The multiple aspects depicted on this board would generally involve presentations by four to six people with each update lasting several minutes, followed by questions from other attendees of the workplace walk.

Figure 8.15: Visual Control Board - Multiple Areas

As you can see from the next photo, the audience for this workplace walk was typically quite large and involved people in various departments including leadership team members. These large updates are often used when an area intersects with many other areas. This is an opportunity for everyone involved to get regular updates and ask questions. Workplace walks such as these often involve discussions regarding the best way to remove roadblocks, gather feedback or concerns, and advise those involved in the downstream process of things that will be coming their way.

Figure 8.16: Visual Control Board - Departmental Reviews

As remote work became more prevalent at UP, it was increasingly important to transfer this concept online. Some of the high-level metrics were moved onto electronic visual control boards. Figure 8.17 illustrates one of the electronic boards.

Electronic Visual Control Board

Site	Project Name	Transition Date	Baseline Metric	Metric at Transition	Month 1	Month 2	Month 3	Month 4	Month 5	Month 6
Elko	***	2/28	181	114	63	82	73	45	85	81
Evanston	***	3/1	21	0	0	0	0	0	0	0
Nampa	***	3/12	3.01	2.80	3.65	2.75	2.80	2.80	3.47	2.72
Pocatello	***	4/2	3.05	2.92	2.93	3.59	2.80	2.91	2.91	2.86

***Project name not disclosed due to company confidentiality

Figure 8.17: Electronic Visual Control Board

IMPROVING IMPLEMENTATION—WHAT TO DO

How Can the Change Initiative Be Improved?

The final question in the iterative implementation plan asks you to consider how you can improve the initiative. You may decide to keep your change team in place for the improvement activities within the initiative, or you may decide to use another team to follow through with the improvements. A complex Change Initiative in a complex organization may easily take more than a year to bear fruit. Therefore, you should consider the timing when determining who will be involved in improving the initiative.

It is critical to invest the time to review the feedback from the various inputs and steadily improve the initiative.

Sustainment after Implementation

Eventually, you and your team will complete much of your iterative implementation plan. You will have improved the Change Initiative, and it will be widely implemented. In our experience, given the early sustainment activities that the Change Questions encourage, the likelihood of your initiative failing at this point is small. In other words, you have probably already beaten the average success rate of most Change Initiatives.

Before the change team has disbanded, you will want to consider removing the ability of people to go back to the old way of doing things. For example, after implementation of a new IT system, the old one is often eliminated. The same goes for things such as new titles, new organizational structures, new billing systems, new HR policies, new promotion criteria, and new benefit plans.

Conversely, there are some change implementations where it is not advantageous or feasible to completely eliminate the old system, making it possible for people to go back to the old way of doing things. A Lean initiative such as UP Way is an example of this. Other examples may include a new leadership program, certain types of process changes, and new ways to interact with customers. Once you have validated that the new system is in place and working better than the old system, if you can't eliminate the old way of doing things, you may want to keep the progress checks in place for a longer time than you would have if the old system was eliminated.

IMPROVING IMPLEMENTATION—HOW TO DO IT

Improving Implementation

*A*t UP, we implemented the UP Way in multiple iterations in hundreds of small and large site activities over several years. After the initial learning trials, we were launching or monitoring the UP Way at approximately fifteen sites at a time. We disbanded the change team fairly early in the implementation process and we gave ownership for tracking and improving the UP Way to the CI department. The group tracked the progress checks in each new area approximately six months to one year after implementation.

In some situations when we revisited these UP Way implementation sites a year or two later, we noticed that although most sites continued with UP Way as an active part of their business operations, some did not. We began to think about how we could mitigate the risk of a late failure after the successful implementation of the initiative. Many of the mechanisms that our change team put into place, such as management system/structure and leadership behaviors, helped to maintain the change, but we needed to do more to ensure prolonged success. We describe the actions we took in the next section.

Failures and Measuring Sustainment

We visited the sites that were lagging in UP Way sustainment. Instead of condemning or shaming the leaders, we endeavored to find out why the sites had failed to sustain the UP Way. Each area needed a slightly different approach or countermeasure. Some sites needed better deployment of LSW, others needed coaching on UP Way tools to more effectively use them and get better results, and finally, in some sites, the leader who was responsible for sustaining the UP Way did not fully understand that he/she was also answerable for sustainment.

The CI team used this information to provide extensive coaching and mentoring to targeted areas. We then developed company-wide methods that not only helped us sustain the UP Way but also gave us a good understanding of our overall success rate. This methodology allowed us to actively measure sustainment of the UP Way at every site. At the beginning of this book, we discussed a 90-plus percent sustainment metric—the method of calculating this rate came from these activities. The new sustainment solutions that were implemented involved:

- Defining the sustainer role,
- Creating the sustainer maturity matrix,
- Creating an escalation process for metrics that were going in the wrong direction, and
- Jointly creating performance goals for the sustainer and mentor.

The Sustainer Role

The sustainment activities described here were put into effect approximately 1-2 years after the launch of the UP Way. Almost all the early efforts within the initiative were of the "carrot" type such as recognition and praise, rather than the "stick" type such as shaming or reprimanding. After several years, we found that it was necessary to use a combination of positive reinforcement and escalation actions with consequences because in some cases positive reinforcement wasn't effective in and of itself. We'll describe some of the methods that were implemented later in this chapter.

When we originally trained employees in the UP Way, we named the person who owned the process where it was being implemented—usually the leader—as the process owner. After the process owners and their teams were trained in UP Way tools, we assigned mentors who worked with the teams for a few months to help them get started. We found that in some locations, the mentor became the quasi-leader of the launch because the process owner abdicated responsibility to the mentor for implementing and sustaining the initiative. Once the mentor left, the initiative often languished.

We used UP Way problem solving tools to develop the following solutions:

- Language is powerful, so we changed the name of "process owner" to "sustainer" so that the person who owned the process clearly understood that he/she not only owned it but was responsible for sustaining UP Way within the process.

- To better define and develop the role of the sustainer, we created a sustainer maturity matrix.

- We also changed the name relating to the timeframe when the initiative was fully implemented. We had previously referred to this timeframe as the "closure." The mentor usually visited the site regularly until the implementation was complete. We decided that closure sounded like the team and the sustainer were done and could walk away. We changed the name to "transition" referring to the fact that the mentor was no longer there to assist, and the responsibility of sustainment and improvement fully transitioned to the sustainer.

The Sustainer Maturity Matrix

During our analysis of why change implementations failed to sustain we realized that we needed to invest more time into focused mentoring around shared development goals relating to the initiative. To do this, we created a matrix.

Sustainer Maturity Matrix

(Partial Example – More categories/rows are included in full matrix)

Focus Area	Level 1	Level 2	Level 3	Level 4	Level 5	Level 6
Problem Solving	Fire fighting	Reactive problem solving	Personal proactive problem solving	Teaches direct reports to solve problems	Encourages cross-functional, proactive problem solving	Problem solving teams are employee led
Data Driven Decisions	Usually determines solution without using data	Recognizes the importance of gathering process data	Can analyze and interpret data	Regularly uses data to make data-driven decisions	Teaches employees to use data in decision making	Employees are skilled in using data to make data driven decisions

Figure 8.18: Sustainer Maturity Matrix

The maturity matrix was used as follows:

1. *When the UP Way was launched at a site, the sustainer completed the map as a self-assessment indicating where the sustainer felt he/she generally performed in each row, indicated in dark green.*

2. *The sustainer then identified where he/she would like to be before the mentor left the site, indicated by dotted lines.*

3. *The sustainer and mentor met regularly to review the matrix, update, and discuss areas that were not meeting the sustainer's goals.*

4. *When the sustainer met the identified goals in each category (row), the mentor left the site.*

5. *Measurements continued on all ongoing UP Way improvement activities for a period of time as described in the next section.*

Escalation Process

In addition to the sustainer activities, we created an escalation process for activities that were lagging. Before the UP Way was launched at a site the escalation process was discussed with and agreed upon by the sustainer.

The Escalation Process Steps

When the UP Way was launched at a site, the first improvement activity was chosen. A key metric was identified for that activity. In general, the improvement activity encompassed a process that had a KPI that was reported monthly to top management as a regular course of business.

Once the process was chosen and UP Way improvement activities were completed, the key metric would be reviewed according to the following steps.

Escalation Process and Sustainment Metric
Calculation Defined

1. If the metric is red* for one month, the mentor asks the sustainer for the reason.
2. If the metric is red for two consecutive months, the mentor determines the root cause with the sustainer.
3. If the root cause is not due to a special cause,** the mentor coaches the sustainer.
4. If there are three to four months of red, the situation is discussed with the CI VP and sustainer's manager.
5. If there are five to six months of red, the situation is discussed with the COO (who reviews metrics monthly).

   * Red is defined as a monthly average that is worse than the average when the project was completed (metric at transition).

   ** Special cause is a circumstance outside of the sustainer's control such as the weather or a derailment. If a special cause occurs, the project sustainment timeline is extended for the length of time it takes to resolve the special cause. The project clock starts over, and the project must have six consecutive green months before the tracking stops and the project is considered sustained. Green equals a metric that is at or better than it was at the project's close.

As our good friend, Jim Morgan, former engineering and operating executive at Ford Motor Company and electric vehicle maker Rivian, is fond of saying, "It's OK to be red, it's not OK to stay red." (Read more about this in Morgan's and Jeffrey Liker's book, Designing the Future: How Ford, Toyota, and other World-Class Organizations Use Lean Product Development to Drive Innovation and Transform Their Business).

Most of the KPI metrics were obtained electronically which made the reporting automatic and easy to track. The COO formally reviewed the KPIs on a regularly scheduled basis. The CI team kept its own measurement system showing UP Way sites that launched. The site metrics were displayed on an electronic/online visual control board and discussed monthly with the mentors within the CI department. The following chart shows a subset of one of the visual control boards. The project names are not disclosed due to company confidentiality. At any given time, we were tracking at least 100 improvement activities at various sites.

Visual Control Board: UP Way Monthly Sustainment Tracking Metrics

Site	Project Name	Transition Date	Baseline Metric	Metric at Transition	Month 1	Month 2	Month 3	Month 4	Month 5	Month 6
Elko	***	2/28	181	114	63	82	73	45	85	81
Evanston	***	3/1	21	0	0	0	0	0	0	0
Nampa	***	3/12	3.01	2.80	3.65	2.75	2.80	2.80	3.47	2.72
Pocatello	***	4/2	3.05	2.92	2.93	3.59	2.80	2.91	2.91	2.86

Figure 8.19: Visual Control Board: UP Way Monthly Sustainment Tracking Metrics

Definitions:

■ **Transition Date**: This was the date that the initiative met its metric goal as identified within the progress check that aligned with the expected value.

- **Baseline Metric**: *This is the metric or KPI that was critical to the initiative. The metric was calculated at the start of each implementation. It was usually an average of the prior twelve months.*

- **Metric at Transition**: *This was the actual value of the progress check metric when the initiative met the goal. We often used a one-month average rather than just one data point to ensure that we actually met the goal, and it wasn't just an outlier.*

- **Monthly Metric**: *The monthly metric was electronically populated at the end of each month. Red indicates that the metric was worse than when the improvement activity was transitioned. Green indicates that the metric was the same or better than when the project was transitioned.*

As an example, if our team reviewed this board, we would have determined that both Elko and Evanston had sustained their improvement metrics for six months. Therefore, they would be removed from the tracking system and would be labeled "sustained." Nampa and Pocatello would continue to be tracked until there were six consecutive months of green. The following chart shows an example of next month's tracking board for Nampa and Pocatello.

Visual Control Board: UP Way Monthly Sustainment Tracking Metrics (One month later)

Site	Project Name	Transition Date	Baseline Metric	Metric at Transition	Month 1	Month 2	Month 3	Month 4	Month 5	Month 6
Nampa	***	3/12	3.01	2.80	2.72	2.80	2.80	3.47	2.72	
Pocatello	***	4/2	3.05	2.92	3.59	2.80	2.91	2.91	2.86	

All Metrics Shifted

Next Month's Metrics

Figure 8.20 – UP Way Monthly Sustainment Tracking Metrics - One Month Later

Individual Performance Goals – Sustainer and Mentor

The change team, with top leadership support, added annual performance goals for both the sustainers and the mentors. The sustainers were given the goal to sustain their UP Way activities for a minimum of six consecutive months, and the mentors had the goal of an annual overall sustainment rate of 92 percent for UP Way projects they mentored.

As the leader of the Change Initiative, I also had an annual sustainment goal of 92 percent for all UP Way activities across the company. Once each site completed its first UP Way activity, the sustainer would identify at least one to two more UP Way activities or projects that would impact key performance metrics. Once those new projects transitioned, we added them to the tracking sheets, as well as the performance goals of both the mentor and the sustainer.

Calculating Sustainment Metrics

Given that the performance goals of many people were dependent upon these metrics, it was critical that the metrics were free from bias and falsification. The majority of the metrics were on auto feed with no human intervention. The overall sustainment metric was calculated annually (the percentage of projects that sustained for six months). The sustainment percentage started in the low 80 percent range when we first began these procedures and steadily improved to a high of 96 percent over several years.

Practical Application: Improving the Change Initiative

It is said that overused strengths can become a liability. We found that out with the problem solving aspect of UP Way. The eight-step problem solving process was an excellent way to address tough, complex, and stubborn problems. However, once people got good at completing the eight steps, the process was used for all kinds of problems, even those where the solutions were fairly self-evident. Rather than quickly solving the straightforward problems, the eight steps were taking extra time and were slowing down the resolution of simpler problem solving activities. What had started as a strength was quickly becoming a liability when addressing straightforward problems.

Ryan, one of the specialists in the CI department was working with a service unit that was led by Vincent. Vincent was frustrated with the speed of some of the problem resolutions in his service unit. He was happy that they were finally solving the big problems, but he felt that the eight-step problem solving process was being overused. Ryan and Vincent worked together to develop a streamlined problem solving process. They named it "seek and solve."

Seek and solve focused on the four steps in the PDCA process. It was often accompanied by brainstorming and implementing small experiments with the idea that if the activity was going to fail, it should fail fast and small. Vincent and Ryan would get the stakeholders together with the employees who were doing the work to do a "go and see" where the problem occurred and try to solve it together. They also gave guidance as to which problems might need the eight steps and which needed seek and solve.

Seek and solve would not have been developed if Ryan had not listened to the internal users of the UP Way. Rather than being defensive about the eight-step problem solving process being the only way to do things, Ryan worked with Vincent to help meet his needs. Seek and solve quickly spread throughout UP, demonstrating that the iterative improvement to the original implementation plan was much needed. The average time to complete the eight-step problem solving process from start to results was six months. The seek and solve process averaged one month with some problems taking as little as a week. Some of the results of the seek-and-solve activities are as follows:

■ Dwell time at a certain location averaged 2.16 hours. The crews needed to print paperwork before each run. The printer was relocated for easier access. Standard work was created for the crew-call process so that outbound crews were ready to board when the train arrived. After the changes were implemented, the dwell time was reduced by 14 minutes per train.

- *The average six-month run time of trains in a particular location was 3.27 hours. After viewing the track and brainstorming with the crews, the crew change location was moved by 250 feet and a test loop was relocated, resulting in a 16-minute improvement in run time.*
- *The average time for certain trains that needed a service activity was 3.01 hours in a particular location. The team analyzed the work events and made changes such as refining standard work and utilizing a previously unused track for service during peak time. The service activities were reduced by an average of 17 minutes per train.*

John's
NOTES

This chapter may be the most valuable one for you as a leader. You and those around you probably have ample experience with creating and implementing plans. But, as the saying goes, "no plan survives first contact with the enemy," where the "enemy" is often simply the real world. Just as there is no PDCA without the "P" (plan), there is no value in a "P" without the "DCA"—doing and checking, studying, reflecting, and acting/adjusting according to changing conditions. PDCA entails continual follow-up, an unending cycle of learning, adjustment, and adaptation. This is usually where the entire change process becomes difficult and where the wheat of change separates itself from the chaff.

In the *Corporate Culture Survival Guide,* Edgar and Peter Schein liken organizational change to a beach with endlessly shifting sands. You implement a given change, then the next waves roll in, the winds shift, and you've got a newly reconstituted beach to contend with. For those of us who inhabit the beach, we don't simply establish one construct and walk away; we *continually* revisit our *continually* morphing constructions. Or as the Lean sensei Kiyo Suzaki puts it, "Winds never stop shifting. When they do, we trim our sails."

When we struggle with sustaining—with the implication or assumption that we did something good, so we think that next we merely need to maintain (sustain) that goodness—we may be working with a wrong assumption from the start. Of course, we want to sustain our improvements (and Lynn introduces a metric that she has used to show for it), but organizations are always changing; there is no "steady state" in organizations at any time. Organizations, like everything else in nature, are either progressing or declining. But that doesn't mean we can't institute desired change that has lasting, needed impact. When we apply positive pressure to create the desired momentum for each change (or each moment), we create the opportunity for ongoing progress.

What does this mean for leaders? First, it is when things do not unfold as planned or predicted that the role of leadership most comes to the fore. How do we as leaders respond when expectations do not match reality? Do we demand sticking to the plan when it has become clear to the organization that the plan was unrealistic? Or, do we too readily abandon the plan for the next flavor of the month? When we feel our organization seeming to "backslide," we may not be doing something wrong in our failure to sustain, but in how we're going about making the change to begin with. Or, as Starbuck and Nystrom put it:

> **"A well-designed organization is not a stable solution to achieve, but a developmental process to keep active."**

Again, change comes in many forms, large and small, complex and simple, easy and seemingly impossible. Full "enterprise transformation," when it comes to that, is not welcoming of consultant-led 12-point implementation roadmaps. We've found, though, that a question and principle-based approach can be fully situational, keeps ownership where it needs to be (which is in the hands of the people leading it), and *feels* natural rather than force fit. You might even think of it as an unending negotiation between your idealized enterprise versus relentless reality.

There are no shortcuts here. Only leaders who are deeply engaged and who continually assess progress on all fronts will be able to determine when to stick to the plan and process versus when and how to adapt to new and continually unfolding circumstances. The bad news is that this is hard work! (That's why Lynn opened this book with an earnest reminder that "intentional change is not for the faint of heart"). The good news is that this is also exhilarating; this is when we as leaders can benefit personally as we tackle each unexpected situation as an opportunity to learn and grow. Isn't that what we each want?

Summary

Just as we proposed pre-work such as creating a communication plan and progress checks before broad application of your Change Initiative, we also strongly promote some important post-work, as outlined in this chapter. Your change team may not be the owners of all post-work activities, but someone must be clearly responsible for the initiative once it is underway.

For a truly robust transformation, it is important to go beyond just the development of the iterative implementation plan. The engagement of employees at all levels in both the plan and the change itself is very powerful and will not only help the initiative be successful but generate an enthusiasm that motivates people around the change.

Change Questions Guide and Digital Workbook

Making It Real

Whether you have a lifetime of experience leading change in organizations or you are someone who has been asked to lead a major change for the first time, we hope that you will find the Change Questions framework useful in leading successful Change Initiatives. Please do not allow the process to become bureaucratic or cumbersome. Rather, leverage the framework as a customizable method such that you will only answer the Change Questions that are appropriate for your *specific* Change Initiative to develop your own *specific* approach.

This looks like a lot of work, right? You may be wondering, "Is it worth it?" We have learned that the time spent on the upfront work will more than pay for itself in getting traction and in sustainment. Still, you may be thinking, "I don't have time for all of this preparation! We have to change right away." In this case, we would argue that you don't have time *not* to do this planning and preparation work. Given that the failure rate of implementing organizational change is high, the odds are that rushing your Change Initiative without the right preparation will result in wasted time, effort, and cost. You may find it helpful to think of the preparation work in this guide not as separate from but as *part of* the actual work to be done.

It is assumed that you have read *Change Questions* before arriving at this guide, which leads you through the detailed work of using the methodology. The Change Questions themselves as presented in the book represent an integration of the work of Lynn Kelley and John Shook, but there are many ways to go about actually *using* the Change Questions. This guide and the digital workbook represent the way that Lynn uses the Change Questions. You are welcome to these materials if they can assist you, or you can chart your own path through the questions, referencing the book for direction as you go. In either case, go forth and change!

THE CHANGE QUESTIONS

What is your value-driven purpose?

- What is the situational problem you want to solve with this Change Initiative?
- What value will the Change Initiative deliver?

What is the work to be done to achieve the purpose or to solve the problem?

- What work changes are required to achieve the objectives of the Change Initiative?
- Where/how will you conduct learning trials to try out the Change Initiative in advance of the full launch?
- How will you get feedback on the Change Initiative to determine whether it's delivering the value that you expected?

How will you engage and develop employees?

- What tools, resources, and development are necessary for employees to have the capability to implement the Change Initiative?
- What is your communication plan to provide information consistently and proactively to employees/stakeholders about the Change Initiative?
- How will you provide positive recognition that will support the Change Initiative?

How will you establish a supportive management system with the appropriate leader behaviors?

- Does the existing management system support the Change Initiative?
  - If not, what changes can you propose?
- How can leaders demonstrate active and visible support of the Change Initiative?

What are your organization's beliefs, values, norms, attitudes and assumptions?

- Is your organization's culture supportive of the Change Initiative?
  - What actions can you take?

Figure 9.1: The Change Questions

The Iterative Implementation Questions

Once you've defined the needed change, you will:

Create and manage an iterative implementation plan
- How can you best implement the Change Initiative with iterative loops for feedback and improvement?

Support and improve your Change Initiative
- How will you gain employee/stakeholder feedback and ownership of the Change Initiative?
- How will you improve the Change Initiative?

Getting Started: Lynn's Approach to Using the Change Questions

If you have picked up this guide without reading *Change Questions*, you may find that you need additional guidance in some areas to answer the Change Questions located here. I have tried to make these instructions as user friendly as possible without recreating the book itself. However, it is a balancing act, so if you need more information, please refer to the corresponding areas in the *Change Questions* book.

Now ... let's get started. I have listed some FAQs that I hear when I facilitate the Change Questions methodology.

Team or No Team?

I recommend that you form a cross-functional, highly motivated, and thoughtful team to work through the Change Questions. A team that is intentionally kept small to stay nimble works well. I like to have teams with a maximum of 3-5 people. Throughout the book, we have referred to this team as the change team. One way to keep your change team small but incorporate more voices at the table is to have subteams or people with specific skills/backgrounds who will attend certain change team meetings. You will find information about the types of people you might want to add to subteams or specific meetings later in this guide.

For Change Initiatives that are not complex, it may be possible for one responsible individual to handle the bulk of organizing your team's approach to the Change Questions process. The designated individual would use the framework to engage with stakeholders, obtain answers and understand their thinking, garner leadership feedback, and propose an overall strategy on how to achieve your desired change.

This change team should be formed as soon as possible once the initiative has been determined. The team will work through the Change Questions together and develop the iterative implementation plan for your specific change.

How long does it take to complete the Change Questions?

I wish I could give you a firm answer, but unfortunately, it depends. The planning timeline to work through the Change Questions framework will depend upon several factors, including the complexity of the change. If you have a fairly straightforward change, you can probably work through the Change Questions quickly—perhaps in a week or less. I have worked with change teams who have completed all Change Questions in a rough format in one day. For a more complex transformation, if your team meets once a week with deliverables due the following week, it could take several months or so to lay the groundwork, achieve alignment, and plan the required deliverables and actions.

You may be wondering what level of complexity your change has so that you can anticipate your planning timeline. No single definition can be applied unilaterally. It is also possible that two initiatives that are exactly the same in terms of the change itself may have vastly different levels of complexity depending upon things like the size of the organization, the number of languages spoken, the level of resistance to the change, and other variables. You and your team can consider the variables and barriers surrounding the proposed change and use your best judgment as to the complexity and corresponding planning timeline.

Do I have to follow all of the steps in the Change Questions?

When you move through the Change Questions, you can consider all of the steps involved. However, if your organization already has an approach that covers one step or if that step does not apply to your organization, there is no need to do it. Also, the size and complexity of the change will be a factor when considering which steps to follow. For example, if your change takes place in a very small department with good communication, it is doubtful that you will need a formal communication plan. You will find that each time you use the framework it becomes easier and somewhat more comfortable for your team to move through the steps. You will develop "go to" tools that will help in all future Change Initiatives.

Do I have to do the steps in the order given?

Since all of the areas within the Change Questions overlap and fold back on each other, once you familiarize yourself with the framework and use it once or twice, you will probably feel comfortable jumping from topic to topic in an order that best suits your organization and the specific change you are implementing. A few of the steps build on a prior step, but in practice, I often change the order of the questions as appropriate. For example, if a major training activity will be necessary and the change team has limited access to training professionals, we usually move the capability building portion forward in the process so that training material development does not slow down the implementation.

What is the difference between the guide and the digital workbook?

This is the guide, and it provides you with the following information in a paper format:

- Answers to FAQs on how to use the Change Questions,
- Sample meeting agendas for each meeting,
- Deliverables and after-meeting work to be completed for each Change Question,
- Recommendations on additional people to invite to various meetings (i.e., communications, human resources, and subject-matter experts),
- A brief overview of each of the Change Question elements, and
- Additional areas to consider when answering the Change Questions.

The digital workbook provides you with the following information in an electronic format:

- All of the information referenced in the guide above, plus:
  - Copies of the forms presented in the *Change Questions* book as fillable PDFs for you to complete electronically, print, and share with others,
  - Examples of how to complete each of the forms.

When should I use the guide versus the digital workbook?

It is recommended that you use the guide when your preference is to facilitate the Change Questions in a non-electronic, brainstorming format such as using a whiteboard or flipchart to record your answers. When using the Change Questions in this manner, it will be helpful to have the book available to reference for sample forms and examples.

The digital workbook can be used to facilitate the Change Questions in the following ways:

- On a video teleconference,
- In conference rooms with a display screen,
- Where each person has the digital workbook on his/her laptop to follow along while the scribe records team answers to the questions on a designated laptop.

Is there a charge for the digital workbook?

There is no charge for the digital workbook as it is included in the price of the *Change Questions* book.

Can I save the digital workbook and my answers to the Change Questions to my computer?

Once you use the link or QR code to access the digital workbook, you can download it to your computer. You will type in your *own* answers to the Change Questions and complete the forms provided. You can then save your work to your computer, send your work to others, and print the workbook as desired. You will especially want to share the workbook with others while working through the Change Questions when gaining buy-in, gathering feedback, and getting alignment on your answers to the Change Questions.

Can I edit the digital workbook?

You can edit your own work within the workbook. However, you will not be able to edit the workbook itself.

A Reminder

The Change Questions represent the planning work that is completed before launching your change initiative. So, for example, when the questions cover topics like training, you won't actually be training employees—you will be *developing* the training. In the communication portion of the Change Questions, you won't be communicating the change, you will be planning the communication around the change.

YOUR TURN: ANSWER THE CHANGE
QUESTIONS WITH YOUR TEAM

If you want to use the guide in its paper format, continue reading the guide. If you want to use the digital workbook in the fillable PDF format, skip to page 231.

Chapter 2: Define Your Purpose

People have a strong desire to understand why the organization is asking them to change and to understand the benefit of the change. Some organizations skip the important step of defining the purpose of the change and risk losing engagement. In this section, you will create a purpose statement, define the problem you want to solve with the initiative, and the value you expect to get from implementing the change.

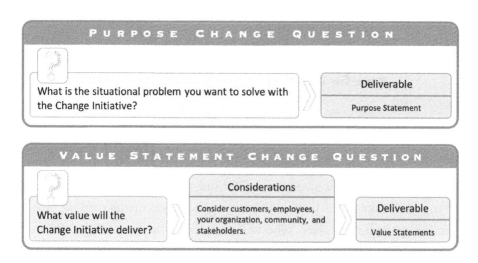

Figure 9.2: Purpose Change Questions

You may utilize the following agenda as a guideline for your meeting.

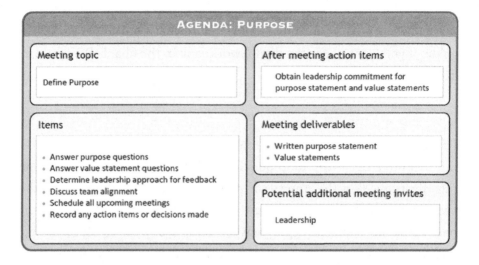

Figure 9.3: Purpose Meeting Agenda

Refer to Chapter 2: Define Your Purpose in the *Change Questions* Book for Additional Guidance and Examples

Chapter 3: Design, Do, and Improve the Work

In this step, you will seek to understand the environment where the change will take place. Once you have a good grasp of the context where the change will take place, who will be involved in the change, the perceptions about the change, design feedback from employees doing the existing work, and the workgroup's existing practices, you can begin to design the new work to be done. You will also determine how you will test the new design and improve it before the full implementation of the Change Initiative.

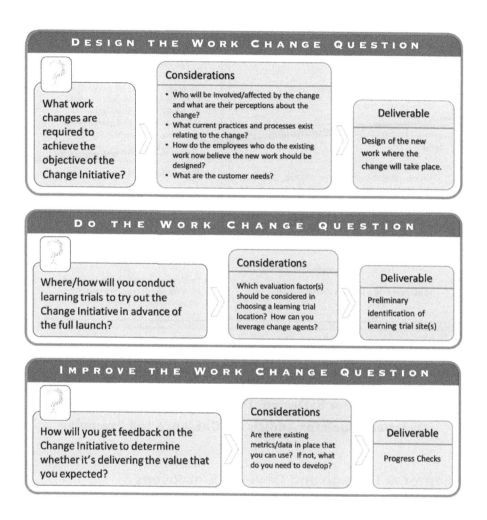

Figure 9.4: Design, Do, and Improve Change Questions

The work of this step generally takes two meetings for a fairly complex change. If you have a very complex change, it may require more than two meetings. For a simpler effort, it may be possible to complete the work in just one meeting.

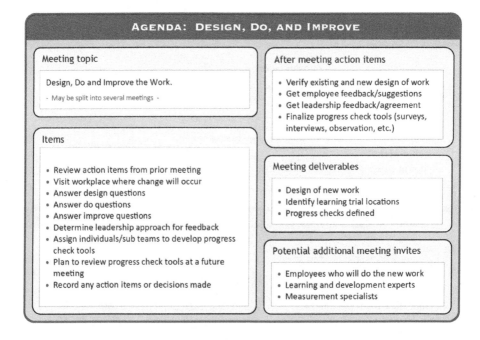

Figure 9.5: Design, Do, and Improve Meeting Agenda

Refer to Chapter 3: Design, Do, and Improve in the *Change Questions* Book for Additional Guidance and Examples

Chapter 4: Engage and Develop Employees

This step of the process encompasses the important aspect of engaging employees in the Change Initiative and developing employees to provide the skills and tools necessary to implement the initiative. In this section we include areas such as building employee capability, through training and development, providing resources, frequent and consistent communication about the change, and recognizing employee successes in implementing the change.

CAPABILITY BUILDING CHANGE QUESTION

What tools, resources, and development are necessary for employees to have the capability to implement the Change Initiative?

Considerations

- Review the work that you did in the "do the work" Change Question
- How should the training be designed and delivered?

Deliverables

- Tools and Resources
- Learning and Development Materials

COMMUNICATION CHANGE QUESTION

What is your communication plan to provide information consistently and proactively to employees/stakeholders about the Change Initiative?

Considerations

- What is the vision for the Change Initiative?
- What key messages support the vision?
- What are the frequently asked questions (FAQ)? How do you address them?

Deliverables

- Vision
- Key Messages
- Communication Plan
- FAQs

RECOGNITION CHANGE QUESTION

How will you provide positive recognition that will support the Change Initiative?

Considerations

- Who should be recognized?
- Which kind of recognition(s) should be given?
- Are there any additional incentives/rewards that will help support the Change Initiative?

Deliverable

Recognition/ Incentive Plan

Figure 9.6: Engage and Develop Change Questions

You will most likely need several change team meetings for these topics. If you are short on time, you may want to split your change team into two groups. One can cover capability building while the other covers communication and recognition with a debrief of both teams' work to ensure the entire change team is aligned with all aspects of the work.

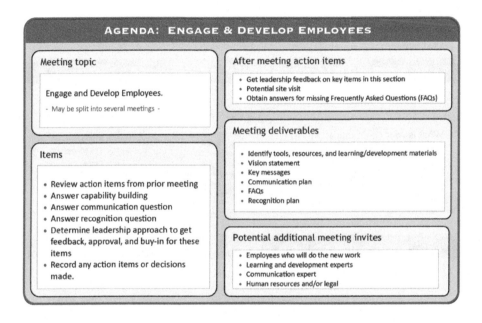

Figure 9.7: Engage and Develop Meeting Agenda

Refer to Chapter 4: Engage and Develop Employees in the *Change Questions* Book for Additional Guidance and Examples

Chapter 5: Establish a Management System and Leadership Behaviors that Support the Change Initiative

We can't emphasize this enough—one of the key reasons that Change Initiatives fail is the lack of a supportive management system and visible leadership commitment. We have broken this area into two parts: (1) management system and (2) leadership behavior that demonstrates a commitment to the change. The Change Questions process helps obtain feedback from leadership regarding their commitment to change and ensure that the management system you have is appropriate to support your change.

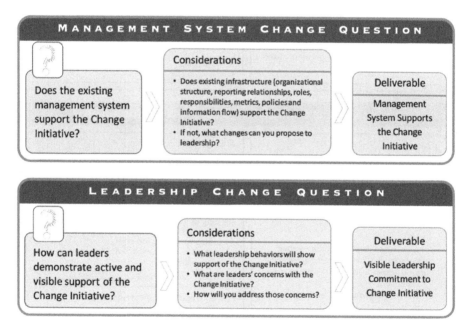

Figure 9.8: Management System and Leadership Change Questions

Notice that this agenda calls for several meetings. During the first meeting, you will design your leadership approach which will include proposed leadership behaviors and possible management system changes. The approach may be guided by feedback from leadership before the first meeting or may be followed by leadership discussions to gather feedback on potential changes. Any recommendations for changes in the management system or leadership behaviors must have buy-in from leadership.

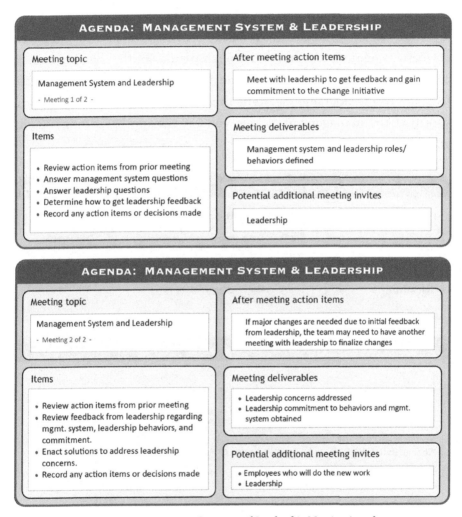

Figure 9.9: Management Systems and Leadership Meeting Agenda

Refer to Chapter 5: Establish a Management System and Leadership Behaviors that Support the Change Initiative in the *Change Questions* Book for Additional Guidance and Examples

Chapter 6: Understand Your Culture

Remember, the central force of organizations is the fundamental *thinking* of the people involved in the organization. This is commonly known as culture. It impacts how the Change Initiative is implemented, the initiative itself, as well as the ongoing success of the initiative. We have depicted culture as central to the entire process in the Change Questions diagram because it influences *all* the other aspects of change. This step is all about helping you understand the impact and importance of considering culture throughout the Change Questions process.

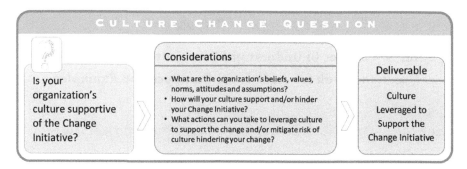

Figure 9.10: Culture Change Question

The amount of time your change team spends at this meeting discussing culture is hard to predict. If your team has a good grasp of your organization's culture, this meeting may go very quickly—especially since you have been touching on various aspects of culture throughout many of the activities leading to this point. If you aren't familiar with the culture of your organization, revisit chapter 6 of the book for ideas on how you can quickly gain cultural insights.

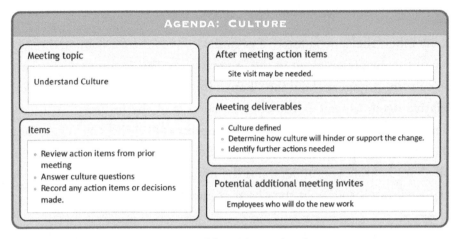

Figure 9.11: Culture Meeting Agenda

Refer to Chapter 6: Understand Your Culture in the *Change Questions* Book for Additional Guidance and Examples

Chapter 7: Create Your Iterative Implementation Plan

The Change Questions work you've completed before this point will come together in your iterative implementation plan. We added the word *iterative* to our implementation plan because we recommend using it to focus not only on the implementation steps but also on the *built-in improvement activities* used to obtain feedback on how to improve the Change Initiative over time.

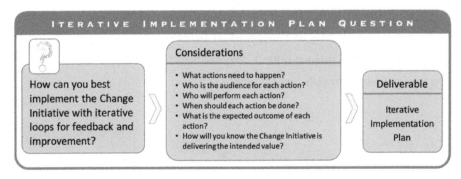

Figure 9.12: Iterative Implementation Plan Question

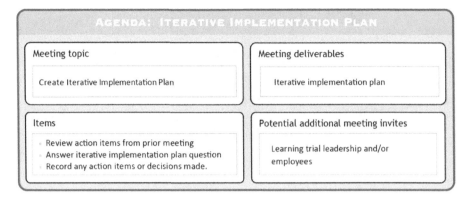

Figure 9.13: Iterative Implementation Plan Meeting Agenda

Refer to Chapter 7: Create Your Iterative Implementation Plan in the *Change Questions* Book for Additional Guidance and Examples

Chapter 8: Support and Improve Your Change Initiative

An implementation plan can benefit greatly from active and planned support. This section presents several examples of ways that you can actively and visibly support your implementation plan to achieve better outcomes.

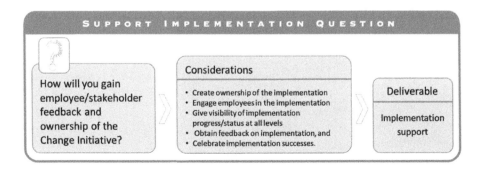

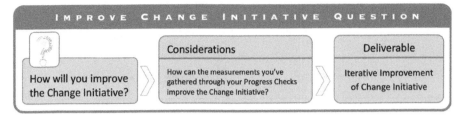

Figure 9.14: Support and Improve Implementation Questions

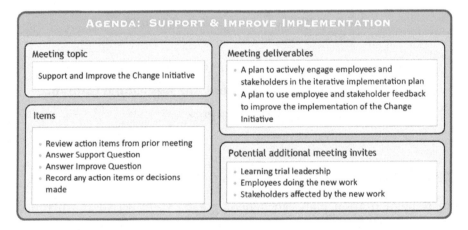

Figure 9.15: Support and Improve Implementation Meeting Agenda

Refer to Chapter 8: Support and Improve Your Change Initiative in the *Change Questions* Book for Additional Guidance and Examples

Using The Digital Workbook

Before your first change team meeting, download the digital workbook by scanning the following QR code or using the link. I recommend that you save the workbook and use it as a living document to track your team's work and progress. The workbook will lead you through the Change Questions process with fillable PDF locations for you and your team to complete for each issue.

changequestions.net

The fillable PDFs in the digital workbook are designed to generate concise answers. If you need more room, you can supplement the digital workbook with your own documents that allow more space, rows, or columns.

Noting Decisions and Team Action Items

In addition to the sections that relate to each element of the Change Questions methodology and correspond to chapters 2-8 in the *Change Questions* book, the digital workbook contains two more sections: decisions and team action items.

Decisions

The decisions section can be used to record every decision made. This will save time over the long run and will reduce confusion during the phase when you and your team implement the change. You have probably served on teams where the team repeatedly revisits past decisions, often because people simply can't remember that a clear decision was actually made—or perhaps because they disagreed with the original decision. This visual recording of decisions will help streamline the decision process.

As you work through the Change Questions process there will be times, however, when it is necessary to revisit some of your team's prior decisions. It's often not easy to discern when a revisitation is unnecessary or not. Sometimes it's in the eye of the beholder. The keys here include alignment, transparency, honest discussion, and, critically, *continually refocusing your attention on learning and working with the facts of each situation*, letting the facts determine your next steps.

Team Action Items

The team action items section is where action items are recorded. You will want to begin each meeting by reviewing the outstanding action item list, showing it on a screen, or distributing it before the meeting. Hard copies can be effective here, although impractical or impossible for remote meetings. Individuals with items that are due by the meeting date will then give a status report on their deliverables. The action list is then updated with the current status of existing deliverables and new action items are added during each meeting. The team action items list is different from the iterative implementation plan. The team action items section is used as an ongoing to-do list for the team to use internally as it plans how to implement the Change Initiative. The iterative implementation plan is used to launch and gain broad adoption of the change.

I sincerely hope that the digital workbook will help you and your team in making the Change Questions come to life!

A NOTE FROM THE AUTHORS:

Remember, this guide and the digital workbook are intended to be used with the *Change Questions* book. We recommend revisiting specific chapters when you aren't sure how to proceed or need to think more carefully with your team.

If you find this guide helpful and want to share a bit of your own organization's change story, contact us at changequestions. net. If you'd like to reach out to us to help you in your use of the Change Questions, you can also reach us through the Change Questions website.

About the Authors

About **D. Lynn Kelley**

Lynn Kelley has worked as a chief operating officer of a hospital, a statistics professor, an executive in the automotive and aerospace industries, and as a senior vice president of supply chain and continuous improvement at UP Railroad. After retiring from UP, Lynn became a senior adviser for Brown Brothers Harriman. Lynn has published several books in the field of statistics and has a PhD in evaluation and research. Lynn's experiences at UP form the basis of the case study in this book.

About **John Shook**

John Shook worked for Toyota for a decade, beginning at the company's world headquarters in Toyota City, Japan in 1983. After helping found the Toyota Production System Support Center in the US, he taught at universities, consulted globally, and wrote extensively. He is the former CEO and chair of the Lean Enterprise Institute and author of *Managing to Learn*, which describes Lean management as he learned it at Toyota, coauthor of *Learning to See*, which brought value stream mapping to wide audiences throughout the world, and of the practical guide *Kaizen Express*.

Acknowledgments

Unless you are expecting an acknowledgment, we are fairly certain that you, dear reader, will ignore this section. If you are still reading, we hope that we give you the credit you deserve. And if, by chance, we fail to mention your name, know that this is only due to our advanced ages and tired brains. We owe you a glass of wine and a deliciously sinful dessert when we next see you (and you rightfully chastise us).

So, on to the business at hand. We owe a world of thanks to the iconic Union Pacific Railroad (UP), where our story takes place. A very special thanks to Jim Young, UP's former CEO who left a remarkable legacy. Thank you to Lance Fritz, UP's current CEO, who had the vision for the UP Way. To that vision and to him we are indebted.

Thank you as well to all our change team members at UP who worked long and hard through the Change Questions and helped convince wary people that the UP Way was more than just the "flavor of the month." Our appreciation also goes out to every member of our continuous improvement team. Our team debated, laughed, collaborated, worked hard, traveled hard, and made a real difference at UP. It absolutely wouldn't have happened without you—O great CI road warriors!

Now ... to name names.

When the book was a mere shadow of itself (and a dismal shadow at that), we called upon three people we respected enormously—Tom Rasmussen, Heather Mason, and Peter Ward—to read the draft and rip it apart. And rip it apart they did (especially Tom). Each of these folks gave us remarkable feedback which helped make the book what it is today. Thank you all.

Our next step was to round out some of the examples we share in the book. Tina Grow, Cameron Scott, and Tom Rasmussen (again) provided the supporting facts we needed to tell the UP story accurately, along with Scott Moore, Clarissa Beyah, John Menicucci, and Tim McMahon who helped keep us honest to ensure that we could use the UP story in the book. Our UP thanks wouldn't be complete without mentioning Denise Prpic who helped with various and sundry details in addition to her "day job."

After two years of writing, we found ourselves floundering—unable to decide on the right structure for our book, what to cut, what to keep, and what, if anything, was missing. Along came our savior/editor, Lex Schroeder who took us in hand and made quick and thorough work of pulling it all together.

We knew we had a match made in heaven when Lex introduced us to Modus Press. Jim Benson and Tonianne DeMaria are kindred spirits who are innovative thought partners and just really good people. Jim and Tonianne introduced us to Olivier Darbonville, our genius graphic designer who is not only creative but amazingly fast, and Susan von Seggern, our publicist extraordinaire.

Big thanks to Mark Shipman from Audivita who worked his magic to effortlessly turn the book into an audiobook. Last, but not least, we extend our gratitude and present the every-*i*-dotted-and-every-*t*-crossed award to our copyeditor Chet Marchwinski, who did the painstaking work of making sure our incomplete sentences were completed and our dangling modifiers were undangled.

Who is left? The people in our lives who support us, love us, put up with us, and give us grief (appropriately!) when the book consumed every waking moment of our days.

Lynn's Personal Acknowledgments

To the love of my life, Daniel Ross. And to our children, their spouses, and our grandchildren who won't be named here as I have embedded your names in this book within the UP story. (Please be advised that the number of times your name appears is not representative of the equal and profound amount of love that I have for all of you!) Krista and Misha - you did an awesome job on making the digital workbook and website a work-of-art.

I am so grateful to John Shook for his remarkable insights, insatiable curiosity, and profound wisdom which helped to guide this book to its current form. John, at times you made my brain hurt as I struggled to keep up with you, but it was well worth the effort. Thanks for being an integral part of this adventure, partner.

Lynn Kelley

John's Personal Acknowledgments

I was flattered when Lynn invited me to contribute to *Change Questions*. I've known Lynn, and observed her success up close, for almost two decades. Not many individuals have the breadth and depth of experience of Lynn as a practitioner/leader. Even fewer have both the emotional/social intelligence and skills combined with an enterprise leader's understanding of the practical need to *get things done* and to lead teams effectively. Lynn gets things done while bringing people along, always making sure to engage people and align the organization so it's a true team effort. Being a part of this project has been a pleasure and a challenge as it brought the opportunity to integrate learnings (the *ways* in which we each leverage the questions and the thinking of how to address them can vary considerably from case to case – but that fact is part and parcel and part of the power of a situational approach) and think together about how organizations can evolve themselves for truly sustainable success. Thank you, Lynn, for all of the positive change you've made happen and for allowing me to contribute to this project.

John Shook

Thank you to our entire team. To all: happy reading, applying, and learning!

Bibliography

1. Intentional Change is Not for the Faint of Heart

Hughes, Mark. 2011. "Do 70 Percent of All Organizational Change Initiatives Really Fail?." *Journal of Change Management* 11, no.4 (December): 451-464.

Taylor, Kory, and Elizabeth B. Jones. 2022. *Adult Dehydration.* Treasure Island (FL): StatPearls Publishing. E-book. Available from the National Library of Medicine, National Center for Biotechnology Information.

Lean Enterprise Institute. 2014. "A Lean Transformation Model Everyone Can Use," January 23, 2014, https://www.lean.org/the-lean-post/articles/a-lean-transformation-model-everyone-can-use/.

Lean Enterprise Institute. n.d. "What is Lean." Accessed March 29, 2023. https://www.lean.org/explore-lean/what-is-lean/.

Luciani, Joseph. 2015. "Why 80 Percent of New Year's Resolutions Fail." U.S. News & World Report (December).

Milkman, Katy. 2021. *How to Change: The Science of Getting from Where You Are to Where You Want to Be.* United States: Penguin Publishing Group.

Nohria, Nitin, and Michael Beer. 2000. "Cracking the Code of Change," *Harvard Business Review* (May-June).

Tasler, Nick. 2017. "Stop Using the Excuse "Organizational Change Is Hard." *Harvard Business Review.* (July).

Wiseman, Richard. 2007. "New Year's Resolution Project." *Quirkology* (blog). Accessed March 20, 2023. http://www.richardwiseman.com/quirkology/new/USA/ Experiment_resolution.shtml.

2. Define Your Purpose

Bartlett, Christopher A., and Sumantra Ghoshal. 1994. "Changing The Role of Top Management: Beyond Strategy to Purpose." *Harvard Business Review.* (November-December): 79-88.

Beckhard, Richard. 1972. "Optimizing Team Building Efforts." *Journal of Contemporary Business* 1, no. 3: 23–32.

Christensen, Clayton M., Taddy Hall, Karen Dillon, and David S. Duncan. 2016. "Know Your Customers' 'Jobs to Be Done'." *Harvard Business Review* 94, no. 9 (September): 54-62.

Doran, George T. *1981*. "There›s a S.M.A.R.T. Way to Write Management›s Goals and Objectives." *Management Review 70, no. 11 (1981):* 35-36.

PwC report. 2016. "Putting Purpose to Work: A Study of Purpose in the Workplace." (June): 5.

3. Design, Do, and Improve the Work

Beckhard, Richard. 1969. *Organization Development: Strategies and Models*. Reading, MA: Addison-Wesley.

Davis, Jocelyn R., and Tom Atkinson. 2010. "Need Speed? Slow Down." *Harvard Business Review*. (May).

Jaworski, Piotr, and Marcin Pitera. 2015. "The 20-60-20 Rule." *American Institute of Mathematical Sciences: Discrete and Continuous Dynamical Systems* 21, no. 4: 1149-1166.

Jones, Renae A., Nerina L. Jimmieson, and Andrew Griffiths. 2005. "The impact of organizational culture and reshaping capabilities on change implementation success: The mediating role of readiness for change." *Journal of Management Studies* 42, no. 2: 361-386.

Lepsinger, Richard. 2007. "Avoiding the Commitment Dip: Seven Ways to Keep Your Employees Focused on and Committed to Change." *Public Management* 89, no. 6: 41-3.

Nadler, D. A., and M. L. Tushman. "A Diagnostic Model for Organization Behavior," in *Perspectives on Behavior in Organizations, eds.* J. R. Hackman, E. E. Lawler, and L. W. Porter, 85-100. New York: McGraw-Hill, 1977.

Rother, Mike, and John Shook. 2009. *Learning to See: Value-Stream Mapping to Create Value and Eliminate Muda*. Boston: Lean Enterprise Institute, Inc.

Schneider, Benjamin, Arthur P. Brief, and Richard A. Guzzo. 1996. "Creating a climate and culture for sustainable organizational change." *Organizational Dynamics* 24, no. 4: 7-19.

4. Engage and Develop Employees

Bersin, Josh. 2012. "New Research Unlocks the Secret of Employee Recognition." *Forbes* (June 13).

Chief Executives Board for Coordination (CEB). 2011, 2015. CEB 2011 Agility Survey. CEB 2015 Employee Change Survey.

Chief Executives Board for Coordination (CEB). 2016. "Making Change Management Work." (February): 3.

Cobb, A. T., K. C. Wooten, and R. Folger. 1995. "Justice in the Making: Toward Understanding the Theory and Practice of Justice in Organizational Change and Development." *Research in Organizational Change and Development*, 8, no 1: 243–295.

Ford, Jeffrey D., Laurie W. Ford, and Angelo D'Amelio. "Resistance to change: The rest of the story." *Academy of Management Review* 33, no. 2 (2008): 362-377.

Jacquemont, David, Dana Maor, and Angelika Reich. 2015. "How to Beat the Transformation Odds." McKinsey & Company Global Survey. (April): 1-14.

Kanter, Rosabeth Moss, Barry A. Stein, and Todd D. Jick. 1992. *The Challenge of Organizational Change How Companies Experience It and Leaders Guide It.* New York: The Free Press.

Klein, Donald. 1976. "Some Notes on the Dynamics of Resistance to Change: The Defender Role." In W. G. Bennis, K. D. Benne, R. Chin, and K. E. Corey (eds.), *The Planning of Change,* 3rd ed. (New York: Holt, Rinehart and Winston, 1976), 117–124.

Kotter, John P. 1995. "Leading Change: Why Transformation Efforts Fail." *Harvard Business Review* (May–June): 58-67.

North, Douglass C. 1990. *Institutions, Institutional Change and Economic Performance.* Political Economy of Institutions and Decisions series. Cambridge: Cambridge University Press. doi:10.1017/CBO9780511808678.

Rousseau, Denise M. 1989. "Psychological and Implied Contracts in Organizations." *Employee Responsibilities and Rights Journal* 2 (June): 121-139.

Satir, V., J. Gerber, and M. Gomori. 1991. *The Satir Model: Family Therapy and Beyond.* Palo Alto, CA: Science and Behavior Books.

5. Establish a Management System and Leadership Behaviors that Support the Change Initiative

Convis, Gary L., and Jeffrey K Liker. 2011. *The Toyota Way to Lean Leadership: Achieving and Sustaining Excellence Through Leadership Development*. New York: McGraw-Hill.

Edmondson, Amy C. 2018. *The Fearless Organization: Creating Psychological Safety in the Workplace for Learning, Innovation, and Growth*. Hoboken, NJ: Wiley.

Greenleaf, Robert K. 2002. *Servant Leadership: A Journey into the Nature of Legitimate Power and Greatness*. Mahwah, NJ: Paulist Press.

Hamel, Gary. 2011. "First, Let's Fire All the Managers." *Harvard Business Review* 89, no.12 (December): 48-60.

Jacquemont, David, Dana Maor, and Angelika Reich. 2015. "How to Beat the Transformation Odds." McKinsey & Company Global Survey. (April): 23.

Lean Lexicon: a Graphical Glossary for Lean Thinkers, 5th ed., edited by Chet Marchwinski. Boston: Lean Enterprise Institute, 2014.

Morris, Randall C. 1991. *The Social and Political Thought of Alfred North Whitehead and Charles Hartshorne*. Albany: State University of New York Press, 1991.

Schein, Edgar H. 1985. *Organizational Culture and Leadership: A Dynamic View*. San Francisco: Jossey-Bass.

Schein, Edgar H. 2013. *Humble Inquiry: The Gentle Art of Asking Instead of Telling*. Oakland, CA: Berrett-Koehler Publishers.

6. Understand Your Culture

Benson, Jim. 2022. *The Collaboration Equation: Strong Professionals, Strong Teams, Strong Delivery*. Seattle: Modus Cooperandi Press.

Drucker Institute, n.d., "Did Peter Drucker Say That?" Accessed Feb. 28, 2023. https://www.drucker.institute/did-peter-drucker-say-that/.

7. Create Your Iterative Implementation Plan

Billi MD, Jack, and Mark Graban. 2018. "Transforming Care: The Value of Lean for Physicians" presentation. *Lean Blog*. April 2018, slide 46 quotes Steve Spear. https://www.leanblog.org/wp-content/uploads/2018/04/May3_16_PCPIWebinar_slides.pdf.

Morgan, James M., and Jeffrey K Liker. 2018. *Designing the Future: How Ford, Toyota, and Other World-Class Organizations Use Lean Product Development to Drive Innovation and Transform Their Business*. New York: McGraw-Hill.

Spear, Steven J. 2010. *The High-Velocity Edge: How Market Leaders Leverage Operational Excellence to Beat the Competition*. 2nd ed. New York: McGraw-Hill.

8. Support and Improve Your Change Initiative

Keyes, Ralph. 2006. *The Quote Verifier: Who Said What, Where, and When*. New York: St. Martin's Press.

Nystrom, Paul, and William H. Starbuck. 2015. "To Avoid Organizational Crises, Unlearn." Research paper posted December 25. http://dx.doi.org/10.2139/ssrn.2708289.

Schein, Peter A., and Edgar H. Schein. 2019. *The Corporate Culture Survival Guide*. Hoboken, NJ: Wiley.

Shook, John. 2020. "Emerging Stronger." The Lean Post (blog), Lean Enterprise Institute. April 30, 2020. https://www.lean.org/the-lean-post/articles/emerging-stronger/.

Index

Made in the USA
Columbia, SC
18 July 2023

20229499R00143